CW01305866

META-HEALTH®

CONSCIOUSLY HEALING YOUR BODY AND SOUL

Susanne Billander

© Susanne Billander 2009.

All rights reserved. No part of this publication may be reproduced, stored in a retrieval system, or transmitted, in any form or by any means, electronic, mechanical, photocopying, recording or otherwise, except as permitted by the UK Copyright, Designs and Patents Act 1988, without the prior permission of the author.

The author publishes in a variety of print and electronic formats and by print-on- demand. Some material included with standard print versions of this book may not be included in e-books or in print-on-demand. If this book refers to media such as a CD or DVD that is not included in the version you purchased.

Designations used by companies to distinguish their products are often claimed as trademarks. All brand names and product names used in this book and on its cover are trade names, service marks, trademark or registered trademarks of their respective owners. The author and the book are not associated with any product or vendor mentioned in this book. None of the companies referenced within the book have endorsed the book.

Limit of Liability/Disclaimer of Warranty: While the publisher and author have used their best efforts in preparing this book, they make no representations or warranties with the respect to the accuracy or completeness of the contents of this book and specifically disclaim any implied warranties of merchantability or fitness for a particular purpose. It is sold on the understanding that the publisher is not engaged in rendering professional services and neither the publisher nor the author shall be liable for damages arising herefrom. If professional advice or other expert assistance is required, the services of a competent professional should be sought.

The purpose of this book is not to substitute medical care in the case of symptoms of a disease. The author does not assume responsibility should patients, based on this book's contents, diagnose themselves without seeing a medical doctor. The book is merely meant to explain and inform the patient from a META-Medical perspective of what occurs in the body during disease. The author works with patients in the treatment of a serious disease only under the surveillance of the patient's own doctor.

English translation: Marina Olsson (www.marinaolsson.se)
Edited by Terry Elston of NLP World

Acknowledgements

I would like to express a deep thanks to the following people, without whom this book would not have come into existence:

Karin Gåvsten, a friend who gave me good advice at a decisive moment of the book writing process. Marina Olsson, for her huge engagement as editor and sounding board. Johannes Fisslinger, president of The META-Health Association. I appreciate him for being a leader of this rapidly growing network. Lucille White, a friend and healer, who checked the vibrational state of the book. Also, Terry Elston, director of NLP World, for his full support and encouragement, and last but not least, my family whom I love deeply.

Contents

Acknowledgements

Preface		1
Introduction		3
Background		9
The META-Health Model		20
1.	**Synchronous Unity**	21
2.	**Traumatic Life Events - Beginning of a Disease Process**	23
3.	**Subjective Perception: Body and Environment as Feedback**	25
4.	**Disease as Process – The Major Points and Phases of a Disease Cycle**	27
	A Disease Process in Two Phases	29
	A General View of the Two-Phase Process	31
	Normal Health	31
	Conflict Shock	31
	Conflict Phase	32
	Conflict Resolution/Soulution	32
	Regeneration Phase	34
	Healing Peak	35
5.	**Brain – Over-Determined Computer Relay for All Organs**	45
6.	**Symptoms – As Biological Meaningful Reactions**	49
7.	**Self-Healing – Responsibility and Life Energy**	51
	Cause and Effect	52
	Finding the root cause with META-Diagnosis	55

	Creating a Bio-Psycho-Spiritual-Social Health	63
	What to do in an Acute Situation?	65
8.	**Spirit – Bio-Psycho-Social Health Through Knowledge and Awareness**	71
9.	**The Process to assist a Soultion**	81
10.	**An in-depth look at META- Health Survey of the Brain Layers**	87
11.	**Microbes – Biological Helpers**	99
	APPENDIX 1 The Underlying Cause Of...	103
	... Metastases	103
	... Cancer of the Brain	106
	... Chronic Diseases	107
	... A Trigger	107
	... Secondary Gains	109
	... Diseases that are Genetically Inherited	110
	APPENDIX 2 CANCER AND THE SOCIETAL DEVELOPMENT	115
	Post Script	121
	About the Author	123
	Training In META -Health	125
	Testimonials	127
	References	133
	Organ-Conflict Directory	134

Preface

One day a boy witnessed a butterfly struggling to get out of its cocoon. After a while he decided that it needed help so he fetched a pair of scissors, cut the cocoon open and expected the butterfly to fly away. But it didn't. When he took a closer look he could see that the wings of the butterfly were not developed, and that it was unable to fly.

He later understood that the whole purpose of the butterfly's struggle out of the cocoon was that mucus would be formed; developing the wings to make them ready for flight.

If we were to draw parallels from this experience with our lives we could say that:

- If we wish to become stronger, we will welcome challenges to overcome so that we can grow stronger.
- If we wish to soar in life, we will run into opportunities to challenge the height of our goals.
- If we wish to become rich in essence, we will encounter situations where it will be possible to create riches, even if only the basic materials for digging are supplied
- If we wish to become high-flying, creative individuals, we will meet people - either positive or negative, with whom to practice our abilities.

How would you experience your life if you did not interpret setbacks as problems, but as gifts helping you to evolve as a human being?

Introduction

How important is Your Health to You?

There are so many things we want in life. Some of us dream of money, loving relationships, success and more time for our loved ones or for what we really want to do. Whilst people who are unwell only have one wish - to get better!

Many of us worry that we, or our loved ones, might become seriously ill. This fear originates from our state of understanding that is totally unable to predict when it might happen. We tend to settle with having certain ideas about what might cause a disease. I would like you to take a moment and think about what you believe could be the cause of a disease. Feel free to write it down in the space below. When you have read this book you can return to this page, and see how much you have learned since you wrote those words.

_____

_____

_____

Think about the word "dis-ease". What does it really mean? Originally it was a word describing a state in which a person did not feel at ease, or was not in a state of "flow". There was a need to label the meaning of a feeling or movement. Later we started using the word as a noun (label), indicating a thing or a state, in order to make it easier to talk about. To say to yourself "I have a disease" is the same as giving yourself a disease sentence. The word gives us an impression of something definite, which is set in stone. It becomes even truer when we get this disease sentence from an authority (a GP or a medical specialist), because it sounds so definite. To us, they know what they are doing. Therefore we often give credit to them when we are worried and have uncomfortable symptoms in our body. What we forget here is that doctors work with disease, not the resources that the body use in a 'repairing' stage of a disease. To focus on disease is good in order to understand the problem. By doing this we can understand the conflict itself. That is a good start, but not a soul...ution. Let's stay in the notion of disease for a moment.

To make it even more filled with "dis" we label disease with even more not understanding labels. Latin names that describe the symptoms we are suffering from, make it even more frightening. They make the disease sound even more complicated than it is. And this is the winner for the disease. Now we give the response...ability to someone else! That 'disables' us to have any ability in our responding body and keeps us in a circle of disease. I fully understand that it feels burdensome to walk around with amoebic dysentery[1] or acoustic neuroma[2]. These are words that most people do not understand.

Now we can choose. Do we still need this *not* understanding circle that 'unables' us to find the answers, or are we ready to bring this disease knowledge to a higher understanding, where we look at the disease and solve it by taking responsibility subconsciously and consciously?

That vaccine is called *Life* and that is already in us whatever state we are in. We might just be ready for that. My question is also: Do we really have any other options in a world that is blooming with physical and mental diseases? I will now share my experiences I have as a Meta-Health coach. The purpose of this is to let you know there is vast knowledge out there when it comes to disease. A knowledge that understands disease on all levels, an understanding that gives us the understanding that brings us back to focus on our being... Life.

Would it be valuable for you to learn about the natural principles of diseases? These are the processes that we are going through at different levels in order to re-establish the balance in the body.

If you answer "Yes" to this question, then this book is for you! META-Health is about using the knowledge from medical art and taking it a step further to actually solve the issue, rather than moving it forward with medicine. It looks like we have a time limit here that is closing up. We seem to not be able to move it forward for much longer. We need the knowledge of disease to allow a shift in theory within medicine, a new way of looking at disease and healing.

I would like to say that META-Health is revolutionary information. It is about taking all the valuable information we have, getting that together and leaving behind what is not working. It is all about evolution in a right direction, spreading information to those who want this incredible knowledge in order to take part in it - so in a way it's about equality.
With the knowledge of META-Health, anyone can take responsibility for his or her own health. My view is that it's all about natural evolution.
And on another level, we all have a pituitary gland and a pineal gland in our bodies. The relationship between these glands allows us to manufacture any chemical/substance we desire within ourselves. So the evolution I am depicting here is one of internal completion of cycles of life that have a relation to our inner beings. When these events/processes are completing, our ability to produce healing substances is apparent.

1) An infection of the intestinal tract causing severe diarrhoea with blood and mucus, caused by a protozoan (amoeba) of jelly-like consistency.

2) A slowly growing benign tumour arising on one of the vestibular nerves.

How I was First Introduced to META-Health

I will never forget the day a respected colleague of mine, Terry Elston called me and told me about a course he had attended. Knowing he is a consultant to the UK government and works with huge companies around the world, made me sit up and listen to an idea about health and healing in an exciting way. Even before I heard all of what he had to say, I could suddenly feel all my cells in my body vibrating, my heart beating quicker and I was feeling a sudden liveliness. He eagerly explained that the course was about natural principles that explained the biological primal (that events have a dramatic effect on the body) cause of cancer and other serious diseases. Very soon, I understood that I had been given information that was as revolutionary as when we had to shift to the reality of the fact that the Earth was round and not flat!

My colleague explained what caused cancer and diseases. He also gave me a brief understanding how conflicts and organs work within us: I started reading everything I could about the principles on the Internet and they echoed as true to me as my knowing that tomorrow is a new day. It suddenly became crystal clear to me how these principles resonated with the methods I already had been using to help people heal themselves.
Ever since I was a child, health issues have been an important part of my life. First, as the saying goes, "You are what you eat". Then as an NLP Master Practitioner I got a deep understanding of the body-mind connection. For me it was not logical that cancer starts developing when a nasty cell starts to divide, the explanation that the Bonnier Medical Dictionary gives us.

I attended the first certified training course in England and felt that META-Health was completely in line with the purpose of my life; and I really felt I wanted to train others in this revolutionary area.

When I normally do what is right for me everything happens easily, but for some reason it was difficult for me to get people to register on my first training course. That is why I started asking myself if this really was the right path for me. When I was having my most serious doubts about the whole thing, something happened, which I interpreted as a sign telling me to carry on. I attended a two-day workshop where a Polish man talked about these principles. He said that there was a movement slowly spreading throughout Europe and that it was going to be a medical revolution. My body reacted again in the same way as when I first heard about these natural laws. At that moment he looked straight at me, and said that I was to start the medical revolution in Sweden! From that day on I have never hesitated: Two weeks later I had my first training session in META-Health with 12 people attending.

International META-Health Association

In 2004, META-Health was founded by a group of medical doctors, natural medical doctors and health consultants. Their purpose was to spread the knowledge of the principles that apply to health and disease, certifying Meta-Medical health consultants and further research.

Meta-Health is based on a bio-psycho-social model of integrative medicine. The Patient and providers work together to develop a diagnostic and therapeutic program that draws on a variety of traditions, expertise and modalities (traditional, complementary, alternative) to address an individual's specific needs (integrative medicine).

The International META-Health Association determines and controls the standards and quality of META-Health training and education. It is responsible for the accreditation and certification of all META-Health instructors and health professionals worldwide.

The Purpose of this Book

I am already actively training people internationally and many participants attending my classes have been asking for written material. Since there was none, I saw it as a natural step to meet this need. I am pleased to spread META-Health knowledge to those interested in learning about it.

I have written this book with joy. A joy that comes from finding a model that underlies a natural system of biological truth. It's not a dogmatic truth, it is the truth of us revealing, awakening and expanding. META-Health is a model that seems to work and resonate within the laws of nature as well as the human evolution.

The META-Health model is helping us identify where we are in a process of life - how that becomes a conflict and where finally the conflict creates a dis-order that is followed by a labelling dis-ease.

The disease is only there as a guide to show us where to find the dis-ease cycle and it also helps us to clarify where we are in our own development.

This model is not only explaining how to get back to health, which for many people means getting rid of the irritating or painful symptoms. It will enlighten habits that have trapped us in negative patterns and caused the disease process to be so uncomfortable, instead of working as a guide to intelligence.

This book isn't just for those who would like to get well and still keep everything the same. We need to dare to take the next step towards responsibility. For example "Help me with my breast cancer, but I am not going to change the way I relate to my husband, even if it helps me." This book is for those who would like to awaken themselves on all levels and create health on all levels.

It is up to everybody to question, reconsider and see the synchronicity about the events that happen in life and the symptoms in our body. I am asking you to analyse the information I am giving you in this book and watch your own illnesses and those people around you. Be observant and test for yourself how this could be true for you? I am convinced because the model turned out to be true in every single case I have applied it to.

My diagnose processes have been shortened considerably. Therefore, I have been able to help my clients realise and therefore enable them to release the primary cause of a problem without wasting unnecessary guessing time.

Part of what we will analyse here will be difficult to assimilate because the subject is so controversial to those who have only been spoon-fed out-dated medical doctrine over many years. The proof of this model is out there already, yet it's hard to find these reference points and case studies. I have therefore chosen to give you references where I am able to. Most of what I show you here can be proven by yourself. So I will ask you to follow me on a journey of understanding life in a way you might have not have done before. And the result of that will meet you with true eyes: The simplicity of life's healing signs and properties.

We will take a look at the medicine of the future and what it could look like. I will not try to persuade you, I will only ask you to keep an open mind. If the future is like what I am going to demonstrate to you here, then we will be able to move forward with medicine and healing in a way that, for some of us, is unimaginable today!

Background

META-Health is not a new practise, as for century's, Chinese medicine and other ancient cultures used a mind-body diagnostic plus an event-body prognosis. That's where we originally got the term dis-ease from.

Even though we can trace META-Health back through time passed, we still have to mention work that has been carried out in our contemporary evolution of mind-body science.

The most recent documented contemporary diagnostic is from the controversial Dr. Ryke Geerd Hamer's original theories, which he called "The New Medicine".

Hamer has had some very bad press, yet we need to

include his work if not for anything else but for historical purposes. The story below also is an excellent metaphor of the bio-psycho-social model.

Doctor Hamer's son, Dirk Hamer, was accidentally shot dead at the age of 17. He died in his shocked father's arms for whom this was obviously a very unexpected and traumatic event. This happened in 1978. Six months later Dr. Hamer discovered that he had developed testicle cancer, despite the fact that he had been well all his life. In his capacity as a medical doctor, he started investigating the possibility of a connection between the testicle cancer and his son's tragic death. He had access to multiple female clients from which to learn about his own dis-ease. Female ovaries correspond to male testicles. He asked these women if they had received any shocking news in their lives anytime during the last two years before they had been diagnosed with ovarian cancer. He discovered that almost all of them had lost a loved one.

After having seen this connection Dr. Hamer started investigating the background facts of different cancer patients. After 20 years of research and after having seen more than 31,000 patients; he was able to establish that serious diseases start with a conflict shock for which we are totally unprepared.

The diseases that the conflict shock leads to are not errors by nature, which we could be tempted to believe - but they all have a biologically meaningful purpose. Mother Nature has designed programmes or principles with the aim of helping either the individual or the group to survive. The programmes work in exactly the same way for humans, animals and plants.

The META-Health network has taken a fresh look at old health teachings and also Hamer's model, arriving at META-Health which is the diagnostic tool. We have expanded the approach of how to recreate health using an integrative model. That means META-Health is including traditional medicine, complementary and alternative medicine, in order to restore health on all levels. If you understand where you are in a disease process; then you can choose the treatment that supports the natural process.

The META-Health Concept – A Definition

First of all we start defining the word Medicine. Medicine is the art and science of healing. It encompasses a range of health care practices evolved to maintain and restore health by the prevention and treatment of illness.

The META-Health concept can be explained using the following three words:

1. META
2. Holistic
3. Biological

1. META

The word originates from Greek and means "over or beyond". A meta position is a position outside a situation, where one can reflect and get perspective. It is what the artist does when he has been working on a detail in a painting, and then takes a few steps back to look at it from a distance. From the distance he can see how the detail fits into the whole picture, or in a bigger perspective. META-Health is not a new therapy or method for treatment, it is a model that biologically and scientifically explains the disease process.

2. Holistic

META-Health does not only include the physical body, but also the mind and soul. We will be discussing not only what happens in our lives but also about our thoughts and values about what happens. Thus, we see an occurrence as something good or bad.

META-Health integrates all medical areas: traditional,

complementary and alternative medicine (see picture below). It is a platform for co-operation between the treatment areas. All therapies have gifts for different parts of the disease process. The idea is to understand the biological process and choose therapies and treatment, which gives support.

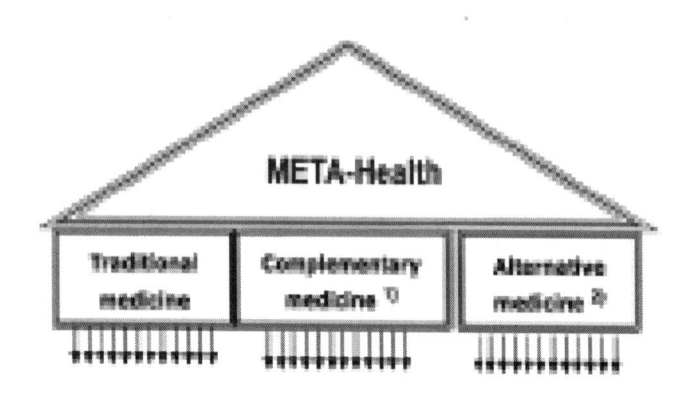

```
                    META-Health
    ┌─────────────┬─────────────────┬─────────────┐
    │ Traditional │  Complementary  │ Alternative │
    │  medicine   │   medicine 1)   │ medicine 2) │
    └─────────────┴─────────────────┴─────────────┘
```

1) The term "complementary medicine" is used today in Sweden to indicate that authorised medical staff (GPs, nurses and so on) are also using alternative medicine such as acupuncture and zone therapy.

2) Alternative medicine is what the western world considers not scientifically proven, even if it were documented in languages other than English. The concept describes holistic medicine that takes into account the whole individual, a medicine that has been used in countries like India or China for over thousands of years with proven results and which does not require expensive resources to be applied. In the Western developed world, pharmaceuticals and surgery are widely used. Seventy per cent of people on the Earth are primarily using 'alternative' medicine.

3. Biological

META-Health is based on natural laws. It is important to understand the difference between a theory and a natural law.

Theory or Natural Law

A theory based on comparing studies and assumptions is usual. For example we say that genes govern and affect our health.

A natural law is a phenomenon where, when repeated, we will always receive the same result. An apple falls down, and not up from the apple tree. We could repeat the procedure showing the same result in 100% of cases. Therefore, it is a natural law.

The fact that genes control biological functions in our body is a known assumption. But what contradicts this theory is that it is possible to extract a nucleus from a cell and the cell can continue living for two more months without this affecting its functionality, according to Dr. Bruce H Lipton. Dr. Lipton is a researcher in cellular biology and author of several books on the subject. (*Biology of Belief: Unleashing the Power of Consciousness, Matter and Miracles*). *We will get back to this.*

Earlier in the book I asked you what you thought was the reason for diseases. Below you will find the most common answers from various participants of my two-day training courses.

- Genetic reasons (due to heredity)
- Contagiousness (viruses and bacteria)
- Wrong kind of food intake
- Lack of exercise
- External influences (such as radiation)

Now let us discuss the above to decide if they are natural laws or not. Do they occur in 100% of cases? If they do, they are natural laws, if not they are not.

Genetic Reasons for Diseases

One often hears about hereditary diseases whose origins are genetic. Researchers have proven that we do not have to become ill just because we have a bad gene. The bad gene only means that we stand a higher risk of developing a certain kind of disease. We could say that the gene is our weak spot. Already before the disease has developed the bad gene was there – but the person was healthy. The question is what activates the bad gene? This is what I intend to explain later on in this book.

Contagiousness

If a person enters a room where there is an influenza virus present, will everybody in the room become infected? No, normally only a few do. Tuberculosis, which is known for its deadly contagious bacteria, does not infect everybody. Everybody who has had sexual intercourse with an HIV-positive person will not be infected. Therefore contagiousness is a theory, not a natural law. The interesting part is to understand why a person can become infected. We will discuss the biological tasks of the microbes later in this book.

The Wrong Food Intake

The film *Super Size Me* showed us that the principal character's laboratory test values were deteriorating because he ate fast food at McDonald's three times a day for one month. Today we know that a daily intake of vitamins and minerals is important to ensure that the bodily processes work and we stay healthy. But there are people who smoke, drink and eat the wrong kind of foods and who are still healthy and feel fine.

Lothar Hirneise who works at The National Foundation for Alternative Medicine in Washington is the author of the book *Chemotherapy heals Cancer and the World is flat*. This is how he explains it. Imagine our body as a huge tank that needs to be filled with energy every day, comparable with the fuel tank of a car. Contrary to cars, human beings have three possible energy sources which they can use. Those energy sources are nutrition, life energy and our feelings! If one source does not work properly we can use energy from the other sources. If a person eats fast food, smokes and drinks and still feels great, then the other sources, such as the life energy or his feelings must compensate for this behaviour.

Japanese researcher Masaru Emoto travels the world and demonstrates how water molecules react differently depending on which feelings have been projected onto them. If a person projects loving thoughts onto the water, the water molecule becomes indescribably beautiful and harmonious, like a snowflake. But if a person projects negative thoughts toward the water molecule, it turns out less beautiful with angles missing. These findings are interesting because they can be applied to food and our bodies. Everything we eat contains water and 70% cent of our bodies consists of water. This means that if we appreciate the food we are eating – whether it is healthy or not – our thoughts will create beautiful or ugly crystals in the food and in our bodies.

It is however easier for many people to absorb nutrition through a healthy diet than from prayer or meditation. As long as we can keep the energy we need every day we will stay healthy. But if we are surrounded by negative people, negative thoughts and we eat fast food, we can be quite certain that we will get ill in some way. Thus, the fact that our food intake can cause disease is not a natural law.

Previously, when I believed in the saying "You are what you eat" I used to read many books about vegetarian and living food. I was really convinced that food, other than vegetarian or living food was harmful to the body. This became a major conflict within me, because I enjoyed other foods and goodies. After a year I became hypersensitive to wheat. My body reacted by not being able to digest food that I *believed* was unhealthy. The hypersensitiveness to wheat disappeared when I solved the conflict within myself. I understood that what I eat in appreciation, my body would handle without any negative consequences.

Lack of Exercise

If a person breaks an arm and walks around with the arm in plaster for six weeks, we know that the arm will lose muscles and become weak. When we train the muscles they become strong again. But there are other factors that have to be taken into account. I can take myself as an example. In one period of my life I used to force myself to exercise 4-5 times a week so that I would not gain weight. I have never had so many problems as I had during that period of time. Why was that? Based on the self-insight I have today, I can say that the reason I was running was because I wasn't comfortable with my body. This means that I was running in a negative feeling, which in the long run caused my periosteum (bones in the lower legs) to become inflamed. During the last two years I have hardly exercised at all, because I travel a lot in my job and consequently don't have time to exercise. Also, I enjoy travelling and when I do, I feel like I am on vacation. Having been inactive has not stressed me in the least because I have had positive feelings. I haven't gained weight, and I have never felt as good both physically and psychologically.

So, it is important to consider one's thoughts in the equation if lack of exercise gets negative consequences or not. Therefore, we cannot consider this a natural law.

External Influence

We often hear people talk about high mortality rates and increased cases of cancer following the escape of radiation from the nuclear power plant in Chernobyl, but this has not been confirmed by further research. Out of the 600 people who were close to the reactor area the night of the

Chernobyl accident on April 26, 1986 134 individuals were acutely damaged due to radiation. 28 people died within four months due to complications caused by radiation, and out of the 106 survivors 11 more people died between 1987 and 1998. (Source: SSI report 2001:07 by Leif Moberg). Moberg also writes that The United Nations Scientific Committee on the Effects of Atomic Radiation, UNSCEAR, which investigated the health effects after the Chernobyl incident, reported an increase in cases of cancer of the thyroid gland between 1987 and 1998. Among those who were born after 1987 the number of cases of cancer in the thyroid gland was considerably less than among those who were born before 1987. This means that the radiation had no increased effect on them. UNSCEAR has not been able to demonstrate an increase of either leukaemia or other tumour related diseases. There has also been talk about inherited effects due to radiation damaged genital cells, but genital cells damaged by radiation have never been detected in humans. The UNSCEAR study continues to confirm that radiation has no proven connection with diseases like metabolic disturbances, neural diseases, problems in the digestive apparatus and depression. What has been demonstrated, however, is that stress following deteriorated social and economic conditions will lead to an increase in a number of diseases.

How is it possible that the same radiation can affect people in different ways? We will discuss this under the section "Subjective Perception".

In closing, I would like to establish that all the usual reasons for what we believe causes disease are theories or suppositions. They are correct in some of the cases but not in 100% of the cases.

The META-Health Model

The META-Health model consists of 10 principles of which principles 1-6 are based on natural laws and which are evidence of disease as a biological meaningful process. Principles 7-9 will describe how one is to go about to create a bio-psycho-social health.

Each principle builds on the earlier one. When you have gone through all of them you will understand the whole. So do not worry if you do not understand everything in the beginning of the book. It is like life itself; sometimes you need to take a few steps backwards in order to understand a seemingly incomprehensible situation. When you look back everything falls into place. Facts will be mixed with examples, case studies and exercises. Also, there is The Organ Directory at the end of this book where you can find out which conflict lies behind which health problem.

1.
Synchronous Unity

Ever since the 15th century, the Westernised view of the human being has been influenced by the view of Descartes. Descartes was a great mathematician as well as a philosopher. He brought about the discussion on *dualism* with regards to body, mind and soul. Even though he said that the soul (spirit) had different 'rules' to the body he saw the role of the Pineal gland in the body as the "seat of the soul". Today, that notion has been taken (probably too much) literally as health care is dividing the human being into separate parts and there are specialists for different parts of the body. Physical and psychological diseases are treated separately. We can illustrate this with three individual circles.

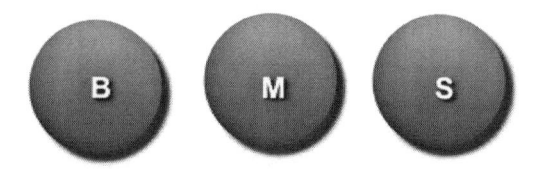

In META-Health we think holistically. It is now demonstrated that everything happens simultaneously. This means body – mind – spirit is a synchronous unity which can be illustrated below.

How this is possible is explained in depth by Deepak Chopra's 1986 book *Quantum Healing*. He is describing scientifically how the link between body and mind works. When two neurons communicate, an electric signal is sent from one neuron to the other by means of a neurotransmitter, a substance that earlier was thought to exist only in the brain. Chopra brought into play the knowledge of neurotransmitter pervading the whole body.

This means that each thought we have, has the possibility of influencing all the cells in the body simultaneously. If we think positive thoughts that give us positive feelings. they will affect every cell in our body. Vice versa, if we harbour negative thoughts that cause negative feelings, they will also affect every cell in the body.

In this model even the environment is included. A problem can only exist in relation to something/somebody in the environment. Read more about this in the section "The underlying cause of a trigger". The next principle will explain how a disease starts and how it affects the whole unity.

2.
Traumatic Life Events – Beginning of a Disease Process

Every disease begins with an unexpected conflict shock. It can be a strong emotional event of major importance to us. Metaphorically we can say that the conflict is not predictable, and it hits us like lightning from a clear blue sky. Usually the conflict shock affects the personality. The individual feels they cannot or do not want to talk about the event, and it can make them withdraw from others. The event may also suffer from a lack of appropriate language to express the issue at the time.

A conflict shock:

- Is unexpected
- Is highly emotional and dramatic
- Isolation of the feeling (a way to protect us from feeling the pain)
- Affects the personality

The conflict shock affects the brain the moment it occurs. It becomes visible as circle formations on a Computerised Tomography (CT) scan1.

On the scan below you can see distinct circles, which are created by what I believe to be frequency changes in the area of the brain affected by the shock.

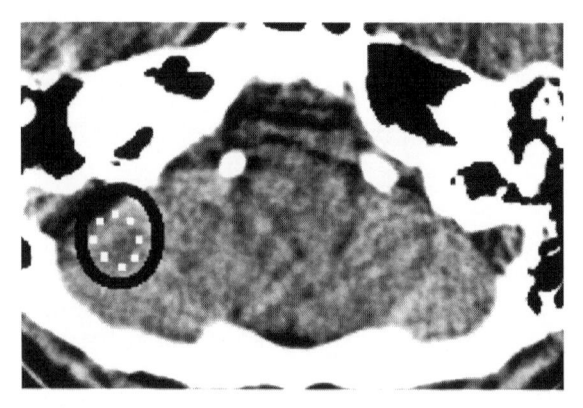

The brain distributes information, conducts and connects our body. The shocking conflict appears as a thunderstorm in the corresponding place in the brain. It then is downloaded downwards in the body through the neural paths, focusing exactly on the organs connected with exactly the area in the brain that was affected. In other words, when the frequency is changed in one part of the brain, the information to the organ or the tissue governed by that part is also changed.

The Body – Brain – Mind unity is affected simultaneously at the moment of the conflict shock. The process occurs simultaneously at all levels from the moment of the conflict shock, until the moment the conflict is resolved and the healing process is completed.

On the CT-scan above the ring would explain that the woman was in a Regeneration Phase of breast cancer, mammary gland, and had experienced a worry conflict with her son.

1) Computerised Tomography; CT-scanner = a device which directs a narrow X-ray beam at a thin section of the body from various angles, using a computer to build up a complete picture of the cross-section

3.
Subjective Perception: Body and Environment as Feedback

What exactly determines where the "lightning" will strike in the brain? The meaning we give to a special event, in other words, what we experience within ourselves at the precise moment an event occurs (the moment of conflict) determines in which part of the brain the "lightning" strikes and thus, which organ will be affected. Events in the mind, brain and the organ occur simultaneously from start to finish, from the very second the event occurs until it is solved.

The interpretation of our situation that we are making at the precise moment of a conflict shock is never objective. If a woman, for example, finds out that her husband is cheating on her, it means objectively that her husband is being unfaithful. Subjectively, it means that we make an unconscious interpretation of what happens. The woman could for example say to herself, "I am not sexually good enough", "I have lost him", "We're going to separate" or, "He has just lost a valuable asset in his life; I am worth something better and there are many others to choose from." The first three thoughts would probably create a negative emotion whereas the last one would not do it. It would come from a person with a strong self-image.

We Cannot See Reality Objectively

Mihaley Czechmihaley explains the background to the above claim in his book Flow in a very understandable way.

He says that about 2.3 million information bits are rushing towards us every second (these figures do vary depending on the researchers – all we need to know - it's a lot!). The brain processes and filtrates the information (generalises, distorts and deletes) through our memories, values, chosen truths, attitudes, our personality and so on. The remaining information quantity is only about 134 information bits, which is comparable to a person being able to keep 5-9 things in their head every moment. (See picture).

Human Communication Model

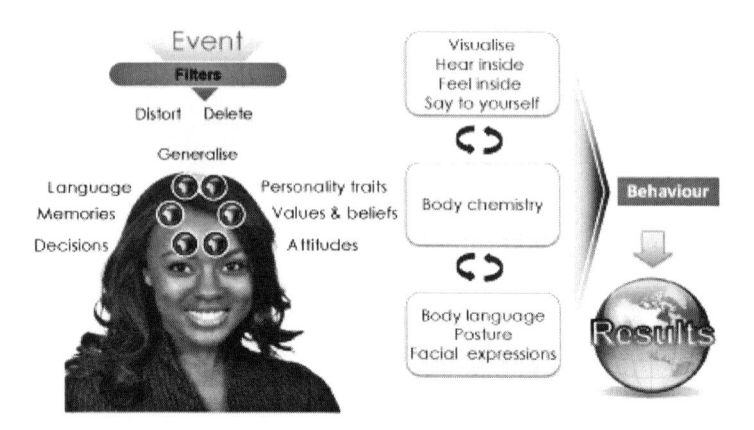

This means that the interpretation we consciously or unconsciously are making at the moment of conflict is a direct reflection of what we already consider true in our inner world. In other words, the body is feeding back to us directly what is happening in our inner world.

Example of a subjective experience and how it affects the brain and the body:

A woman discovers that her husband has been unfaithful and a conflict shock arises.

Subjective Meaning	Affected Brain Layer	Affected Organ
"I am not good enough"	Cerebral Medulla	Bone
"I cannot digest it"	Brain Stem	Stomach
"This means separation"	Cortex	Breast Ducts

4.
Disease as a Process – The Major Points and Phases of a Disease Cycle

Our world consists of opposite poles where one does not mean anything without the other. For instance plus – minus, up – down, man – woman, day – night, light – darkness, active – passive. The rhythm between the poles creates life, nature and the cosmos.

In the same way, the disease process consists of two phases. Before explaining the fourth principle in this section, which is about a disease process in two phases, I will give you some basic knowledge about the sympathetic and the parasympathetic nervous systems.

The autonomic nervous system

The autonomic nervous system is the part of the nervous system that functions without us being conscious of what is happening and without our conscious will is able to manage it.

The autonomic system is divided into the sympathetic and the parasympathetic part.

The sympathetic has contact with the entire body, while the parasympathetic part does not affect our blood, fat tissue and skin.

Overall we can say that increased sympathetic activity puts your body in "flight or fight" mode, while increased parasympathetic activity favors digestion, excretion of waste products and reproduction.

The two systems are constantly active, but their relative activity ratio varies widely. When a person is at rest, the parasympathetic activity dominates over the sympathetic activity. When this peace is broken, the relationship changes, the sympathetic become more active than the parasympathetic.

This can be seen on heart rate, pulse rate and cold hands/feet. Here it is clear that heart rate increases when you become physically active, but also increases, when the "mental tranquility" is broken (i.e. when you are scared, or when the person you are in love with comes in).

Increased sympathetic activity improves a person's ability to use the body (to work, fight or flight). It facilitates breathing by causing the smooth muscle of the delicate larynx to relax, whereby the larynx becomes more open, and the heart works faster and with more force. Blood vessels to the intestines close, so the blood primarily passes through the muscles, and finally stimulates muscle metabolism. The sympathetic effect is amplified by the adrenal medulla, which produce adrenaline.

Increased parasympathetic activity has positive effects on digestion by increasing the secretion of digestive enzymes, and by increasing bowel movement. This means that there is a large blood flow to the intestines in this situation and particularly increased kidney function. Furthermore, the parasympathetic facilitates the emptying of the urinary bladder.

The parts of the brain that affect the autonomic functions are located in the brainstem and directly above. These brain areas are also of great importance to the unconscious influence of tension in skeletal muscle. Muscle tension increases while sympathetic activity increases, whereas the muscles relax in situations that are characterized by parasympathetic dominance.

Increased sympathetic activity is suitable when the body

must be used. While parasympathetic activity is necessary to "rebuild and clean out" (digestion, defecation, etc.). If a person has stable good health, then there is a good balance between the sympathetic and parasympathetic activity. This implies that we spend our energies during the day where sympathetic is dominant, and afterwards we heal and rebuild ourselves at night when parasympathetic is active.

Let us now see how a conflict shock affects that balance.

A Disease Process in Two Phases

The balance between the two phases of the nervous system will be disturbed if we experience a conflict, which affects us so strongly that we go into shock. At that point we enter a Conflict Phase and the sympathetic phase is more activated in order to provide us with the strength to do something about it. Instead of resting at night we will lie awake brooding and when we do, we do not restore our reserves for the next day. If this situation prevails over a period of time, it becomes like a negative spiral and our batteries will be discharged. If we solve the conflict, we will enter into a Regeneration Phase where we often feel as if our energy was completely gone and we feel exhausted. In the Regeneration Phase the parasympathetic nervous system dominates.

The process of moving through a Conflict Phase and a healing Regeneration Phase is called a disease process. Normal symptoms, which we normally call diseases are; eczema, colds, fever or cancer. According to META-Health they are not diseases, but part of the disease process.

The Conflict and Regeneration Phases, which can be traumatic and lead to disease or less traumatic, encompassing everyday events in our lives, are illustrated in the examples below.

Example 1:
If you cut yourself on a knife the blood vessels react by contracting (Conflict Phase) and the wound turns white. A moment later there is the relaxation phase, the stress lets go and the flow of blood through the blood vessels increases and there is a reddening of the skin.

Eventually there is a normalisation and the wound is healed. The wound might result in a scar, which is nature's way of making the tissue stronger in future.

Example 2:
Most of us have sometimes exercised strongly, which stretches/tears the muscles (Conflict Phase). The next day (Regeneration Phase) our muscles feel sore and exhausted. The muscle needs to rest in order to rebuild itself. After that the muscle grows stronger in order to be able to handle extra strain in future.

The muscles react in the same way if we experience a mental conflict shock where we think depreciative thoughts about ourselves like "How will I be able to cope?" with negative focus on the fact that we might not be able to.

In the Conflict Phase the organism is trying to cope with the burden. At the time of the Conflict Phase one often does not feel any symptoms or strained muscles.

In a Regeneration Phase, one feels the aching muscles because they are in the process of being rebuilt.

Example 3:
When a person starts a new job and has to sort out a lot of impressions, like new colleagues, names, new and known working tasks and so on. They often experience stress (Conflict Phase and strain) during the first week and can be very tired every night (Conflict solving and relaxation).

Medical textbooks previously identified a few hundred 'cold' and a few hundred 'warm' diseases. Patients with

'Cold' diseases present with cold skin and cold extremities; they are in protracted stress, lose weight have difficulty falling asleep and suffer sleep disorders. For example we have cancer, MS, angina pectoris, neurodermatitus, diabetes, mental and mood disorders. Other diseases are defined as rheumatic, infectious, allergic and especially exanthematous (skin eruption).

A General View of the Two-Phase Process

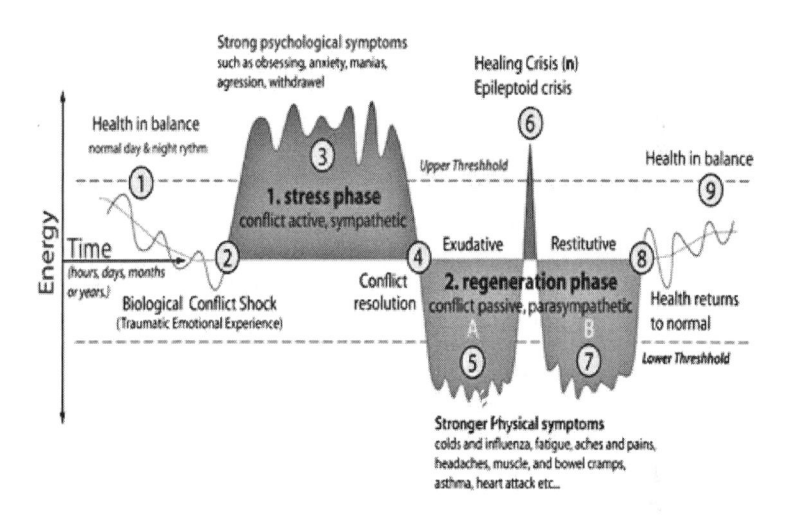

1. Normal Health

Normal health means there is balance between the day's activities and the night's restoration.

2. Conflict Shock

An unexpected, dramatic conflict shock breaks the natural rhythm between activity and relaxation, and it affects the organ-brain-psyche simultaneously. On a CT-scan, circles can be seen on the part of the brain with which the conflict is associated.

3. Conflict Phase

At the precise moment of a conflict shock the body reacts by increasing the options to manage the conflict. It does this by returning to the stress phase. This phase is called the Conflict Phase (the cold phase) and it always follows the conflict shock.
Characteristics of the Conflict Phase:
Body:
- Cold hands and feet
- Higher blood pressure
- Increased pulse rate
- High glucose rate in the blood
- A higher adrenalin rate in the blood
- Suffers from loss of appetite
- Weight loss
- Unable to relax
- The muscular tissues are strained
- Insomnia

There is cell growth, cells are breaking down or a disorder of the organ, tissue or function of the bodily part is started. The process starting depends on which brain layer and conflict the organ belongs to. This is explained in the Chapter 5, "Brain – Over-Determined Computer Relay For All Organs".

Brain:
- The core of the conflict is seen as circles on the part of the brain affected by the conflict.

Psyche:
- Can't stop to think about the conflict.

4. Conflict Resolution/Soulution

If or when a person experiences a resolution of the conflict the process is reversed. A resolution might be that the environment changes - for instance in connection with a change of job or when someone meets somebody new after having lost a partner. The solution can also take place at an emotional and spiritual level, such as when people learn from an incident and heal themselves through those events as a catalyst. I call that soulution.

Example Resolution: If a man, whose wife has passed away, would find himself a new wife, then the substitution means that the conflict is solved at a biological level. Then our system goes into the Regeneration Phase. In this case the regeneration will be as long and intense as the conflict phase. The conflict can arise again if we meet another situation that reminds us of the first conflict. I will explain more about chronic diseases later in the book.

In the META-Health network we established that it is possible to solve conflicts at different levels; in the environment, on the emotional, mental and spiritual levels. This is the soulution.

The focus is to learn from our conflicts in order for us to be able to grow as individuals. This is the same as a physical muscle getting stronger from being stretched. I assist my clients to release negative emotions associated with the trauma they have internally. When a person is releasing the negative emotion then she/he can hear the wisdom of the soul, and the true learning will come through and create freedom in the previous situation. Any kind of therapy that enables the person to stop reacting with an old destructive feeling in situations is the right one. When solving a conflict consciously within you, then the accumulated conflict mass gets released (conflict length and intensity) from the Conflict Phase. That means the equation changes and that the Regeneration Phase can become shorter and easier to go through.

Example Soulution: *A woman in her mid-fifties came to see me. She had unexpectedly been left by her husband and reacted to the situation with a loss conflict. Instead of focusing on quickly finding her another man, I helped her discover what she needed to learn from the situation. She quickly realised that she had the belief "I am not desirable" as a truth about herself in her inner world. When I helped her release the truth she became able to draw to herself a man who did not (unconsciously) have to make the old truth true for her, and leave her.*

5. Regeneration Phase

The Regeneration Phase is the healing process of the disease, which we normally identify as an infectious disease, which is why it is called the warm phase. During this phase the process is reversed since the conflict is resolved. The body switches over to a relaxed phase governed by the parasympathetic nervous system, which is prevailing when you are relaxed and at ease. The purpose of the phase is to restore the balance in the body.

Characterises the Regeneration Phase:
Body:
- Tiredness
- Warm hands and feet
- Higher bodily temperature – fever
- Increased hunger
- Increased weight
- Lower blood pressure
- The organ is starting to recover by breaking down the cellular increase. "Holes" left after cells have been broken down are quickly filled again.
- After the Regeneration Phase the person is back to health again.

Brain:
- The core of the conflict (the circles) in the brain starts to heal. Headache can be present.

Psyche:
- Peace of mind. The person no longer thinks about the conflict.

The Regeneration Phase can, however, be sped up through the use of therapy. The duration and intensity of the conflict and the Regeneration Phase changes quickly when one uses therapy to release the conflict mass in the Conflict Phase. Most of the therapists using Power Techniques are able to assist an emotional release. If negative emotions are released from the cellular memories it becomes easier for the body to recover.

6. Healing Peak

In the middle of the healing phase, when the relaxation is at its peak, a healing peak can occur. The risk for complications caused by too deep a relaxation is at its greatest at this moment, when the tissues are filled with liquids and mucous. The purpose of the healing crisis is to press out all the extra liquid from the specific brain relay and the affected organ. In this crisis the person relives the conflict, which means that the thoughts about the old conflict can re-emerge. It can be explained biologically that the body wants to test if the individual is ready to deal with a similar situation in the future.

After the healing peak, the system goes back to the last part of the Regeneration Phase, where the person normally gets milder symptoms prior to the healing peak. In the case of influenza the healing crisis is evident. First a person feels very ill; after a few days they feel much better and go back to work or out for a walk to get some fresh air. The next day they are in bed again, complaining that they should never have gone out in the first place. Do you recognize the phenomenon?

We call it a healing crisis because symptoms are also (for instance) heart attacks, migraines, epileptic seizures or asthma attacks. These can be life threatening in themselves if the body has been going through a trying period during a long and intensive Conflict Phase, or if the person is not strong enough for regeneration.

That is why we like to assist people to release the negative emotion and the conflict mass from the Conflict Phase to the Regeneration Phase. Then the healing peak can become shorter and less intense.

Disease in Conflict and Regeneration Phase

Often the symptoms of the Conflict Phase look like one disease, and the symptoms of the Regeneration Phase look like another. However, the "conflict phase" and the "regeneration phase" diseases are not individual diseases, but two different symptoms of one and the same process. Often the individual does not feel ill in the Conflict Phase since that is when they are fully absorbed with solving the conflict by fighting, escaping or constantly brooding over the problem. In the Regeneration Phase the individual normally feels quite ill and this is when the visit to the GP normally takes place.

"Conflict phase" Symptom	"Regeneration phase" Diseases
1. Vitiligo (white pigment spots)	Eczema
2. Lung Cancer	Tuberculosis
3. Osteoporosis	Bonecancer, Leukaemia

A deeper explanation of these examples will now follow.

Vitiligo - Eczema

The outer skin layer (epidermis) is what separates us from the external world, which is why we can get symptoms of eczema after a Loss-of-Contact Conflict.

The biological purpose of the Conflict Phase is to make it easier for the individual to cope with the separation; therefore the skin is made less sensitive. The body does this by means of cellular destruction, which turns the skin dry, white and cold. If a person experiences a brutal separation conflict the symptoms turn into vitiligo (white pigment spots) during the Conflict Phase.

During the Regeneration Phase the skin must be repaired and during this process it turns red, inflamed, liquefied and itch. When the ointment cortisone is applied, the skin gets stressed again, moving from the relaxed phase (the warm Regeneration Phase) to the stressed phase (the cold Conflict Phase), so the process repeats itself.

Case Study

A father came to see me with his 12-year old daughter who had eczema covering large parts of her upper body. Her parents were divorced. Ever since the father had moved out, the daughter had been alternating between the parents, staying one week with the mother and one week with the father. The father had a bad conscience because the daughter always had reddening eczema when she stayed with him, but during the week with the mother the eczema healed. Unfortunately, I didn't know of META-Health at the time, but it became obvious to me after having learned META-Health when I thought about her. Since it was the father who had moved out, the conflict was "Losing contact with daddy". The week after (when she was living with her mother) belonged to the Conflict Phase, where the symptoms were less sensitive skin. The week she lived with her father meant an unconscious conflict resolve. Therefore she went into a Regeneration Phase with the reddening eczema symptoms when she stayed with him.

Eczema is very common among small children. Normally it disappears when the child grows older. Children, especially babies, are totally dependent upon their caregivers. Therefore, a separation conflict can be experienced during such an ordinary situation as when the mother puts the baby down to start preparing dinner. The reason for this is that the baby has no conception whatsoever if the mother will be away for a minute or forever!

Cancer of the Lungs – TB

During which two periods of time did Tuberculosis, TB, peak in Europe during the 20th century? It peaked during the First and Second World Wars (one source stoptb.org). It was actually declining rapidly, so why did it then peak during war?

Fear of death is the conflict causing lung cancer. It used to be a normal conflict for men who went to war and even for their relatives. In order for them to be able to fight better for their lives, nature created a special programme helping an individual to increase the number of alveoli in their lungs. These are the cells that absorb the oxygen we inhale. Biologically, it enables the individual to absorb more oxygen and thus have more strength with which to fight. When the conflict was solved, or if the man survived the war, the programme turned into the Regeneration Phase. This helped the lungs return to their original form. At that point the cell growth needs to be destroyed and eliminated from the lungs. The symptoms are coughing up blood, high temperature and exhaustion. The bacteria in the lungs found by the doctors were TB, and according to the prevailing medical belief the bacteria were responsible for the symptoms. I will get back to you with the true task of bacteria when I describe the fourth principle about the Microbes.

Does Smoking Cause Cancer?

There is a lot of talk about smoking causing lung cancer. According to the Cancer Foundation as many as 98% of the respondents in a study believed that smoking had a great influence as a reason for cancer. The paragraphs below are not to encourage smoking at all. Simply that things are not always the way we are 'programmed' to believe. We must all do our research to find our 'truths'. Below I will present research from W. Dontenwill (Journal of Cancer Research and Clinical Oncology).

Thousands of hamsters were put in cages where they were subjected to cigarette smoke. None of them developed squamous epithelium bronchial cancer or a pulmonary (lung) nodule cancer.

In another trial, house mice were used as trial animals. Some of these developed lung cancer (alveoli), which is triggered by a fear of death conflict. The reason why is that house mice have always lived near humans, which has caused them to biologically inherit the premise that smoke is life threatening. Some of the house mice reacted instinctively with a fear of death conflict, and wanted to escape from the cigarette smoke that was blown into the cages. When they could not escape there was a conflict shock among them, so they developed lung cancer.

A hamster is not disturbed (no psyche effect) by smoke because smoke does not exist in his underground burrows, so he has not developed a panic code. Therefore, they have no instinct telling them that smoke means "run for your life".

The research was therefore able to establish that smoking does not cause bronchial cancer, but in some cases it might cause lung cancer (alveoli). This is despite the fact that cigarette smoke does not penetrate as far as the bronchi, and by no means as far as the alveoli.

"In General, Inhalation studies have not found that tobacco smoke leads to squamous cell cincimona of the lung" (Wynder and Hoffmann 1967: Mohr and Reznik 1978; IARC 1986a&b)

Although I am not condoning smoking as healthy and must underline that smoke is toxic and possibly very harmful, I do not also condone the idea that smoking kills in all situations.

If all the above being true, then what is cancer?

The body can react with cell growth; one example is in the case of kick boxers. In practice, they kick each other's shinbones and in order to protect the shinbone the body grows more cartilage. This makes the bone stronger to be able to bear more pain. There is cell growth, but only so much as to strengthen the bone. Every case of cell growth does not equal cancer.

Healthy cells in the body normally divide and increase in number according to a predetermined pattern. The cancer cells on the other hand, have released themselves from these growth laws, and will divide uninhibitedly in the long run causing a cancer tumour (website of www.pfizer.se).

META-Health explains why a cell starts dividing uninhibitedly. A programme is activated after an unexpected, dramatic conflict shock, with the purpose of supporting survival or evolution. If the cell growth happens in a Conflict or Regeneration Phase, it can be explained in principle five.

Osteoporosis – Bone Cancer

The skeleton is the basis and foundation for our body and it will be affected if we find ourselves in a conflict where we devaluate ourselves. We might, for instance, think that we are not good or capable enough, or feel that we are not worthy enough. After a conflict shock involving this kind of content, a cell destruction process will begin in the skeleton. This is the reason for osteoporosis. The stronger the emotional conflict and the longer it prevails, the weaker the skeleton becomes until bone is broken. It is not uncommon for the elderly to break the collarbone in falling accidents.

Different areas of the skeleton are being affected depending on which area we are devaluating ourselves in.

The Head	Intellectual self-devaluation
Throat and Neck	Injustice, moral
Shoulders	Inability to keep somebody
Hands	Inability to act and do something
Thorax	Central personality conflict
Lumbar	Self-devaluation of the core of who we are
The Pelvis	Sexual conflicts
Hips	Inability to withstand a situation
Leg	Inability to stand a situation, kick away someone/something or run away
Knee	Inflexibility, sport activity
Ankle	Inability to run away or move forward

Why are there So Many Cases of Osteoporosis in Sweden?

Below we will list some of the reasons for osteoporosis according to the prevailing medical view of the western developed world.

• Women in menopause create less estrogen, the hormone that helps keep the skeleton strong.
• Some pharmaceutical drugs can cause osteoporosis.
• A person who has been physically inactive for some time easily develops osteoporosis.
• Cadmium can be a reason why osteoporosis is so widely spread in Sweden. This is according to new findings presented by Karolinska University Hospital. Cadmium, which works against calcium in the body, is a common mineral in the Swedish soil. Evidence has shown that women with a lack of iron are able to absorb larger doses of cadmium, which puts them at a higher risk of developing

osteoporosis.

My private reflection: Everybody does not develop osteoporosis despite the fact that all women go through the menopause, grow older or eat vegetables from the soil. The ones who read CT-scans in our network have always been able to detect a frequency change in the Cerebral Medulla when they examine a client with the symptoms of osteoporosis. The frequency changes only come about if a conflict shock involving self-devaluation is experienced. Since only a very small number of physicians have applied the knowledge of META-Health, there are unfortunately not many references in this area.

Again, I do not want you to believe blindly in me, but I encourage you all to become curious. Should you or anybody you know have a tendency towards a weak skeleton I would encourage you to reflect upon whether there could be any conflicts involving self-devaluation within. The Law of Jante1 (a number of unwritten moral rules, according to which the first one stipulates that you should not differentiate yourself from other people by believing you are something special) is very deeply rooted in Swedish culture. This could be a contributing reason for the large number of cases of osteoporosis in Sweden.

1) The Laws of Jante

You must not believe that you are something. You must not believe that you are as good as we are. You must not believe that you are smarter than we are. You must not believe that you are better than we are. You must not believe that you know more than we do. You must not believe that you are superior to us. You must not believe that you are good at anything. You are not allowed to laugh at us. Do not believe that anybody cares about you. Do not think that you can teach us anything.

Jante was originally the fictive name of a small village in a novel by Aksel Sandemose (1899-1965), where the local inhabitants failed to see their hometown's sons and daughters as unique grown-ups with talents and skills. Jante can today in a figurative sense be any environment, workplace, classroom, school, relative, family or gang.

Bone cancer

Bone cancer is the Regeneration Phase of the disease osteoporosis. In the Regeneration Phase, bone has to be rebuilt and when this happens there is aching, there can be inflammation and also swelling. The purpose of the ache is to prevent the bone from activity until the skeleton is healed. Without treatment of skeleton cancer, the bone heals naturally and grows even stronger than before.

Is it then positive to be diagnosed with bone cancer because that would mean one is recovering from Osteoporosis? Well, it might not feel so positive because the symptoms are troublesome, but so too are they when one breaks a leg.

How does the Body function when you break a Bone?

During the healing process the skeleton is rebuilt and it hurts and it becomes swollen and inflamed. Often surplus bone tissue will be created, which is the body's way of making the bone stronger in the future. The process is as natural as the healing of bone cancer. What we often haven't seen is the foregoing osteoporosis, which makes it possible for us to understand the reasons for the sudden cell growth in the skeleton. When one has broken a bone this is the reason for the ache and the swelling.

Case study:

Anitha, 36

Leukaemia

After a divorce Anitha and her son were going to move from South Africa to London. She sold her flat and her furniture, but when she opened her mail the day before departure she discovered that her ex-husband unexpectedly served her with a writ. This was a totally unexpected shock. Since she did not know how long the process would take, she arranged for a temporary flat where she and her son had no furniture. During this phase (Conflict Phase) she was experiencing no physical symptoms, and she was focusing all her strength on solving the problem. The process lasted for two years and finally she won the case, after which Anitha and her son moved directly to London (Conflict Resolution).

Upon arrival in England she started feeling exhausted and listless (Regeneration Phase). After awhile she went to see a doctor who diagnosed her with leukaemia, and told her she had a maximum of three months to live! This diagnosis would have floored anybody, but not Anitha. She refused to make it her truth and started using her own therapy. This was fasting and drinking fruit juices, meditating and visualising health for 21 days. When she returned to the doctor's office to give blood samples she was completely recovered. The doctors could not find any traces of leukaemia in her body.

Biological Reason for Leukaemia

After an unexpected conflict which affects us deeply, (a conflict which we can feel "in our bones"), bone marrow will start decomposing. This causes less red and white blood cells to be produced. A low level of red blood cells creates lack of blood or anaemia.

In the recovery phase bone marrow is being rebuilt and there is dramatic growth of White Blood Cells (Leucocytes), which is what we call leukaemia.

The increased number of White Blood Cells damages the production of Red Blood Cells, which causes the blood value to drop further. Normally the increase in Red Blood Cells (Erythrocytes) happens 4-5 weeks after the white blood cells, which is when production will normalise.

5.
Brain – Over-Determined Computer Relay for All Organs

In the preceding section I gave examples of the process of eczema and lung cancer. You might be wondering why there is cell destruction in the epidermis after a Loss-of-Contact Conflict, and cell growth (tumour) in the lungs after a Fear-of-Death Conflict. The fifth principle will explain this.

In observation, doctors observed that some of the patients developed tumours during the Conflict Phase together with typical stress related symptoms (insomnia, loss of appetite, cold hands and feet). Whereas others, who were diagnosed with cancer, showed evidence of Regeneration Phase symptoms. They had just resolved a conflict when the cell growth started.

They compared these findings and symptoms with each other with the help of X-rays from computerised axial tomography, CT (See explanation on page 24). They then realised that among all of those who had developed their tumours during the Regeneration Phase, the conflict core was visible somewhere in the region of the Cerebral Medulla and Cerebral Cortex in the form of a darkening (evidence of fluid accumulation) with blurry circles (evidence of regeneration). Whereas among all those who had developed tumours during the Conflict Phase, and who showed evidence of these symptoms, the CT showed conflict cores of clear circles (evidence of an ongoing conflict) in the region of the Brain Stem or Cerebellum. There were no exceptions to these processes.

Conflict Phase   Regeneration Phase

All of those who had circular waves as an expression of increased activity in the Cerebral Medulla and Cortex did not only lack every trace of cell growth, but showed, in some cases, destruction of the tissue in the corresponding organs. It was then concluded that the cell growth in the Regeneration Phase in fact, means restoration of the destroyed tissue or organ. The process itself is evidence of this. If the whole process is left alone and the regeneration process is supported with the help of rest and stabilisation, the body will heal itself. Thus, it is not advisable to operate or take samples in such an area during the Regeneration Phase, because that could disturb the regeneration process and provoke a further increase in cell growth.

The Evolution of the Brain1

The brain has developed over the millions of years that the human species itself has developed, which means that the different organs and tissues originate from different parts of evolution. This is why the tissues react in different ways to a conflict. Survival programmes, which are millions of years old, make a certain area of the brain activate itself. Each programme has a basic good intention and is designed for survival and evolution. This is nothing new. Even the well-known biologist Charles Darwin found this out.

The oldest conflicts relate to the Brain Stem and affect the part of the organs governed by it. At the precise moment of the shock the body reacts in order to increase the options of handling and resolving the conflict. This happens by cell growth (cancer tumour), increased hormonal secretion, and increased destruction activities and/or increased strength of the tissue. When the conflict is over the tumour is slowly destroyed during the Regeneration Period, after which the body returns to normal.

1) Ten million years ago when our forefathers and chimpanzees started walking different ways, the size of a male brain was 350cm3. The Homo-sapien species emerged one million years ago with a brain size of about 1,000m3 and 200,000 years ago it had developed into 1,400m3. (Source: Lars Wilsson, Naturlig mat, Optimal förlag, 2006)

Both humans and animals react in the same way to these biological conflict shocks. The conflicts belong to the same symbolic system.

Example:
An animal tries to eat a piece of food to large for it's body that it cannot digest. On another level, a person gets into a conflict with a situation in life that they cannot accept, or digest. In both cases, the body then reacts by creating more cells, in order to be able to produce more stomach juices which will help the stomach to digest the problem. These rapidly growing cells that are created to solve the problem are wrongly interpreted as a tumour and a person is diagnosed as "having cancer".

META Physiology

Often we perceive our body as something we "have" despite the fact that it is a living organism. The German philosopher Martin Heidegger describes it in one sentence: "We are the ones that hear, not our ears." It means that we do not hear because we have ears, but we have ears because we are hearing individuals. Likewise, we have lungs because we breathe. This explains how a conflict that somebody experiences such as "being unable to digest something", stimulates the stomach to start producing more gastric juices that produce cells to help us digest the 'chunk'.

6.
Symptoms – As Biological Meaningful Reactions

The way we normally define disease is not valid anymore according to a META-Medical point of view. If we are aware of the principles we can say that every disease is a special programme by nature with a specific biological purpose. Thus, a disease is not a mistake by nature but a meaningful and intelligent process created by nature that has been developed over millions of years. This gives us an understanding of how we are part of the cosmic interaction for the principles that apply to humans, animals and plants.

Presupposing that the biological purpose is basically survival and evolution, it then seems that the purpose of the biological programme lies in the Conflict Phase when it comes to the Brain Stem and Cerebellum; and in the Regeneration Phase when it comes to the Cerebral Medulla and Cortex.

After conflicts belonging to the Brain Stem and the Cerebellum, the biological programme helps us solve the conflict. When we for instance experience the conflict of not being able to digest something, a cell growth of the cells producing digestive enzymes is started to help us "digest" the conflict. Or there is growth of dermis cells so that we will be better protected after a subjectively experienced attack conflict.

But after a self-devaluation conflict, belonging to the Cerebral Medulla, the skeleton will be destroyed until we have solved the conflict. Only in the Regeneration Phase will the bone be growing stronger. It is as if nature takes it seriously that we do not experience self-worth because of the body mirrors not being valuable (we grow weaker).

In the world of animals only the strongest will survive, and those that are able to adapt to a new environment.

Time and time again we are given the opportunity to realise that nature does not make mistakes. We are talking about a highly reliable order working according to universal principles, quietly and invisibly expressing themselves through the picture created in the material world.

7.
Self-Healing – Responsibility and Life Energy

Is it possible to heal just any disease? The fact that 99% of all the bodily cells are exchanged in a year convinces me that it is possible.

Morris E. Goodman's, *The Miracle Man,* proves that what many people deem to be impossible can actually be possible. Goodman crashed his airplane and survived with a broken spine, a swallowing reflex that did not work properly and a diaphragm that was destroyed. This made it impossible for him to breath on his own. The only thing he could do was to blink his eyes. With the help of blinking he communicated to the hospital staff that he was going to walk out of the hospital by the following Christmas. They considered it impossible. Goodman admitted that it was true that his body wasn't operating at the time, but his mind was. He was convinced that you become what you focus on. He started creating inner pictures in his mind of somebody who was able to walk, and he focused on how it would feel to attain his goal. There was an enormous amount of work and effort behind this, but by Christmas he was in fact able to walk unaided out of the hospital!

If you understand how the body works, you can work with it to restore your health. Please note that you cannot decide exactly how it will work. Luckily there is an intelligence taking care of that. Otherwise we would be busy telling the heart when to beat, the cells to divide, the stomach how to digest the food, and so on.

Since many of us do not understand what happens when the body starts to react with fevers, headaches, diarrhoea or tumours, we often become frightened and suddenly want to decide how the body should work. The fright is a result of our way of thinking about disease and health. We have not learned that body and mind are linked together, which is why we have not learned to ask the questions that leads us to the teachings we need in order to heal.

This is worth noting: If a person is diagnosed with a fatal disease, more than 99% of the body is still functioning. According to statistics, people immediately feel worse when they have been diagnosed than before. This is because they easily start focusing on their disease, and start giving it all their attention until the disease engulfs their whole reality.

If we have a serious disease we still have another choice to make, and that is to take back the power in the disease process. I cannot stress this enough, it is so important. And how do we do it?

We all know the equation cause and effect, which means that something causes the results we are getting. We could choose to think that disease is a result of something, and become curious to find out exactly what created the symptoms in the body. How we are able to arrive at the reason depends on which side of the equation we choose to stand on.

Cause and Effect

If we are afraid of viruses and bacteria, believe that we are a victim for bad genes, or a galloping cell growth that cannot be stopped, then we are standing on the effect side of the equation. If we are standing on the effect side, we will reason without knowledge that body and mind are connected. We cannot understand that the reason and even the resolution (the cure) of the disease lie within us. Since we normally do not have knowledge of our own body we go and see somebody who has more knowledge of it, such as a doctor. At the doctor's surgery we will receive treatment to eliminate the symptoms. Often we are prescribed pharmaceutical drugs or undergo an operation. The thoughts of a person on the effect side normally lead to a feeling of powerlessness "Why did this disease strike me?", "I was unlucky, I got infected...", "What have I done to deserve this?" Feeling powerless is a passive feeling, since we do not believe we can affect the situation in any way.

We need to learn to think in a new way. And this is what we are doing when we are standing on the cause side. The person standing there is open to the concept that the disease has some kind of a connection to the person as a whole. If we are standing on the cause side we are filled with power, since we assume that we have the possibility of affecting the situation. If we got into this problem, we can get out of it.

Exercise

Stand or sit in front of a mirror. Read the four statements below and say them to yourself in a normal voice. (This exercise is perfect if you are working with a client to see if there is resistance to becoming well and what kind of resistance it is).

If you can say the statements to yourself in a convincing natural way, you're fine. If you can't say them, or do not want to, it means there is some inner gardening to do!

1. I can be 100 per cent healthy.
2. I allow myself to be 100 per cent healthy.
3. I am willing to do what it takes to become 100 per cent healthy.
4. I am 100 per cent healthy.

How do you feel when you say these things to yourself or to your coach? How do you react? Note if there are changes in facial colour, voice, body language and inner feeling.

The word **"can"** identifies if you really believe that you can become 100 per cent healthy. There is a saying that belief moves mountains. If there is no belief that something is possible a person will give up, which does not help in recreating health. If that were the case, it could be a good idea to find other people who have had the same disease and who have restored their health and talk to them, or read books about self-healing.

The word **"allow"** identifies if you feel you are worthy of becoming 100 per cent healthy. If you do not feel worthy of it, I recommend you contact someone who can help you get in touch with this feeling. The more we feel we are worthy, the more we allow ourselves to accept riches from the universe.

The words **"willing to do"** identify if you are going to do what it takes to make the needed changes. Here we are talking about the individual's own responsibility. Will I do what it takes to recreate health? If not, what are the secondary gains for me to continue not being healthy? (See Chapter Secondary Gains).

The words **"I am"** identify the prevailing situation. Think about how you would define being 100 per cent healthy.

It is important for you to describe for yourself how you would know that you are in possession of the health that you are striving for. The definition of health varies from person to person. Many people know that they want to become free from their problem, yet they have no clear image of how that will change their life. What would a symptom-free life mean to you? What could you be, do and have that you currently don't?

What would you see, hear and feel if you were free from symptoms? Feel free to take a few moments to contemplate about it and then write it down.

Finding the root cause

As we said before, META-Health is not a new form of therapy or a treatment model. It is a model, which biologically explains the disease process. The purpose of making a META-Medical diagnosis is to become conscious of where you or a client stands in relation to the disease process. Then it is possible for you to see what you can do to recreate health in harmony with the natural process.

In order for us to be able to find the root cause we need information. The disease process consists of seven steps. The process runs simultaneously on all levels (Environment – Nervous System – Psyche – Brain – Organ) from the moment of the conflict shock until the conflict is solved and the healing completed. (See picture below).

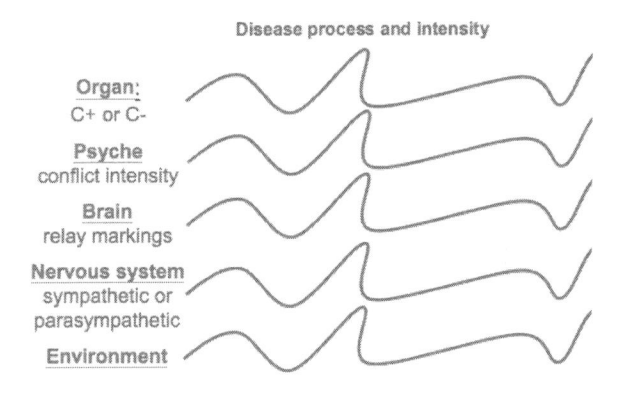

Disease process and intensity

Organ:
C+ or C-

Psyche
conflict intensity

Brain
relay markings

Nervous system
sympathetic or
parasympathetic

Environment

Because of this we have many possibilities of finding information when we are looking for the underlying pattern. The more facts we can come up with, the more exact our diagnosis will be. Since the process runs simultaneously we actually only need information from one level to understand what is happening on the levels we do not have information from. (It could, for example, be difficult to get hold of a computerised axial tomography (CT) if one is not working as a physician).

For every step in the disease process information we can look for information on all five levels.

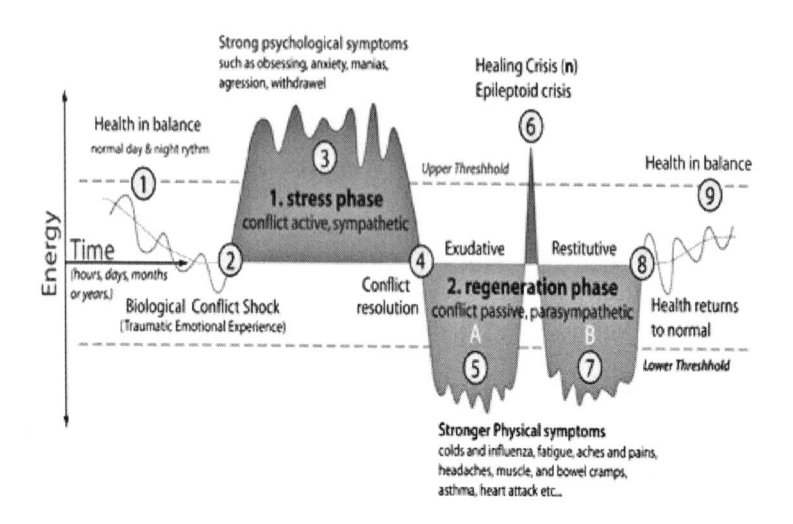

Strong psychological symptoms such as obsessing, anxiety, manias, agression, withdrawel

Healing Crisis (n)
Epileptoid crisis

Health in balance
normal day & night rythm

Upper Threshhold

Health in balance

1. stress phase
conflict active, sympathetic

Time (hours, days, months or years.)

Exudative   Restitutive

Conflict resolution

2. regeneration phase
conflict passive, parasympathetic

Biological Conflict Shock
(Traumatic Emotional Experience)

Health returns to normal

Lower Threshhold

Stronger Physical symptoms
colds and influenza, fatigue, aches and pains, headaches, muscle, and bowel cramps, asthma, heart attack etc..

The Disease Process
1. Normal Health
2. Conflict Shock
3. Conflict Phase
4. Conflict Resolution/Solution
5. Regeneration Phase
6. Healing Crisis
7. Normal Health

The Levels
1. Body – Organ
2. Psyche – Conflict
3. Brain Layer – CT
4. Nervous System
5. Environment

Example:
There are visible facts to look for in the form of symptoms in the body to determine if a person is in the Regeneration Phase. It could be an inflamed muscle, peace of mind after a person has let go of a burden, oedema visible on a computerised axial tomography (CT), or that a person shows evidence of an activated parasympathetic nervous system (warm hands, exhaustion and so on) and that there

possibly has been a change in the person's immediate environment.

Right or Left Dominance

Looking for right or left hand dominance is also adding valuable information when we are diagnosing. Our dominant hand mirrors which part of the brain is most connected to how we associate with conflicts. Also, we can read how a problem on a certain side of the body originates from a certain conflict.

The Clapping Test

Right-or left-hand domination can best be demonstrated by the clapping test. This is how we do it: start by clapping your hands spontaneously, then stop and observe which hand stays over the other. The hand, which is over the other, decides if you are left or right-hand dominated. If you make a neutral clapping, you have to test yourself towards what feels most natural for you.

Right-Hand Dominated   Left-Hand Dominated

Neutral

NOTE – You could be right-handed and still clap with the left hand over the right one, in that case you would be left-hand dominated. Many left-handed people have had to relearn to write with the right hand, but in reality they would be left-handed.

In the case of a right-hand dominated person the right side of the body represents the partner (loving or business partner) or father or siblings. In the case of a left-hand dominated person, the left side of the body represents the partner (loving or business partner) or father and siblings.

In the case of a right-hand dominated person the left side of the body stands for children, mother, and home/nest. In the case of a left-hand dominated person the right side of the body stands for children, mother, and home/nest.

To give you some examples of right and left-hand dominance, I will refer to the lady who had the kidney stone problems who was right-hand dominated. She had a conflict with her partner, which resulted in her right kidney being affected. I wrote about the woman with the cyst on her ovaries. She was left-hand dominated, which made her left ovary affected, since the conflict was about her father.

Whether you are left-hand or right-hand dominated is important for all brain layers except for the Brain Stem.

Cracks on My Tongue and a Blister on the Right and Left Sides

During my first visit to Germany during the diploma training in META-Health, I suddenly discovered that I had a sore spot on my tongue, which I thought was caused by the hard surface of the bread I was eating. During the second part of the training in Germany I got the same symptoms as previously; sore spots on my tongue. I shared my experience with other participants during a group exercise, during which I learned that the surface of the tongue actually was skin, which meant that the symptom of a separation conflict was applicable to me. Biologically the skin is governed by the Cortex and during the Conflict Phase the skin is broken down (C-), which can easily be felt as small cracks on the tongue. When the conflict is resolved the skin is repaired again (C+), and sore blisters appear.

What happened on the biological plane was that I experienced a separation conflict when I left my loving partner Eric, and my home, to travel to Germany. After two days in Germany I decided to accept my situation and to make the best of it, which was when the symptoms of the Regeneration Phase started. Since the conflict was both about my partner and my home, there was a blister on both sides of the tongue.

I asked myself: How come it was the skin on the tongue that reacted and not any other part of the skin on the body? The logical answer was that it was only with Eric that I was able to experience total closeness, and the tongue represented that intimacy to me.

That was the end of the META-Diagnose, but I wanted to learn more from the conflict and grow on a personal plane. I asked myself what I could learn from the situation; the teaching really touched me.

I had associated the feeling of intimacy with Eric. This means that when I left him, I closed down within myself in order not to feel the aching pain as much. No wonder then that I missed him. I was closing myself off from a part of myself, which was the intimacy of my feelings. I really used to feel like an empty shell when I was away. Even when I called him I didn't feel there was any intimacy in our conversations since I had shut my feelings off earlier. This only made the experience of separation stronger. When I was sharing this with my group during the exercises, I could feel how I started opening up again and how a certain softness came over me. I felt like I was coming home in myself and I felt closer to myself. Even the rest of the group noticed my change and commented on it.

Ever since, I am honestly letting myself really feel all the feelings I have when I travel. Now I have learned to be "at home" even when I am away from home.

Think Biologically

If I do not know which conflict lies behind a certain symptom, I always presume that the patient's unconscious mind knows. The trick is to ask the right question to elicit the right answer.

Questions to myself/the other person:
1. What biological task does the organ have in the body?
2. How could the symptom, the organ is exhibiting, be a reflection of what is happening in your life right now?

Example:

Ache in the Membrane around the Peroneal

A man was experiencing ache in the membrane around the peroneal (relating to or supplying the outer side of the leg). He asked me about the reason for the conflict that led to the ache. He felt the ache because the muscle was growing faster than the membrane was growing. I asked him how this situation could be a reflection of what was happening in his life right now, and it became obvious to him. He wanted to train more than his body would allow, as he wanted to be as well-trained as possible for a cross-country running competition. The body directly reflected that he would not be able to proceed faster if he trained more, because the membrane was not allowed the time it needed to enlarge as fast as the muscle did. He then realised that if he rested instead of training he would be able to run better.

Sore Pads

A middle-aged woman had had sore pads under her feet every morning for two months. I asked her what biological task the pads had and she answered, "To enable us to walk comfortably". I then asked her if there had been some kind of change in her life just before the symptoms started? She replied that there had been a change, because she had to go to a new workplace as a measure of rehabilitation. She had nothing against the work itself, but she felt that she was forced to go there, and she didn't feel comfortable about it.

When it dawned on her that the ache had to do with the feeling she was experiencing, she found the motivation to influence the situation. She chose to contact a coach in her hometown to help her release the feeling.

META-Health has proven extraordinarily successful when it comes to understanding the organism and in diagnosing. Once we have diagnosed, the next step is to guide yourself or the patient to the best suitable treatment. Sometimes no treatment is necessary because the body might already be in the process of regeneration. Rest and patience can often be very helpful.

The process to find the root cause of a symptom/ illness

1. What is the symptom? What organ/tissue does it belong to? Even more specifically, what part of the organ/ tissue does it belong to? Find it in The Organ Directory in the end of this book.

2. What is the issue that triggers that symptom/ disease process to start in that part of the organ? Find it in the The Organ Directory.

3. Does the symptom belong to the Conflict or Regeneration Phase?

4. Have you/the client symptoms that belong to the sympathetic or parasympathetic? (Cold or warm hands?, Stressed or relaxed?, Thoughts that are spinning about an issue or calm?, Higher pulse or lower?)

5. If the symptom belongs to an organ or tissues that exist in the whole body what metaphor gives more details to the conflict?

The Head	Intellectual self-devaluation
Throat and Neck	Injustice, moral
Shoulders	Inability to keep somebody
Hands	Inability to act and do something
Thorax	Central personality conflict
Lumbar	Self-devaluation of the core of who we are
The Pelvis	Sexual conflicts
Hips	Inability to withstand a situation
Leg	Inability to stand a situation, kick away someone/something or run away
Knee	Inflexibility, sport activity
Ankle	Inability to run away or move forward

6. Are you/the client, Right or Left Dominant (Do the clap test)

Let me give you an example how to elicit the information and put it together, in order to find a question that will help us discover the underlying conflict.

A right dominant woman who suffered from eczema on the inside of her right arm.

Organ: Skin - Epidermis
Conflict: Loss of contact – separation – conflict
Eczema is a symptom that starts in the regeneration phase. The parasympathetic nervous system is more activated, with symptoms like warm skin, itching, tiredness, inflammation
Metaphor: Not being able to hold on to....
Right Dominant means it has to do with a partner

The question would be to discover the root cause:
Just before you got the eczema the first time, did you get back in contact with someone/something that you at one point unexpectedly and dramatically lost contact with?

I will explain later in the book how to move on from knowing what the root cause is to assist a *soulution* to happen. This means releasing the old pattern, getting the learnings, and re-connect to the resources that then helps to heal the body as well as creating a new life circumstance.

Creating a Bio - Psycho - Spiritual - Social Health

These questions will help you see what practical things you could do to restore your health. The questions below will consider you as a whole: body, mind, spirit and the environment. The result will be an action plan for which you will have to assume responsibility in order to achieve your goal – perfect health.

The Body
Organs
Is treatment necessary?
Are there any alternative treatments to support the symptoms?
Immune System = Vitality = Life Energy
What can I do to improve my life energy?
It is extremely important to support the body and replenish

it with energy so it will be able to cope and restore itself.
Fitness
What can I do to strengthen the body and keep it strong and vital?

Mind
Solve the Conflict.
Identify the conflict. How can I solve the conflict? Who could help me do it?
Find the Trigger.
If we are talking about a chronic process it is very important to answer the question: What actually starts this conflict over and over again, it is something I see, hear, feel, smell, taste or say to myself?
Emotional Balance
What can I do to release feelings and create an emotional balance in my life?

Spirit
Consciousness and Understanding
In what way is this condition perfect for me?
What is the higher purpose of what I am going through right now?

Assume Responsibility for the Situation and for your own Health.
What will I see, hear and feel when I am enjoying good health? What are my health goals?
What positive changes can I make?

The Environment/Surroundings
Real Biological Conflict Resolution
What kind of changes do I need to make in my environment in order to solve the conflict and the triggers?
Create an Environment Supportive to Healing and Health.
Would my surroundings be able to support me in my healing process?
Do I need to make any changes?

What to Do in an Acute Situation?

This is a question many people ask me: what should a person do when they have an acute condition such as meningitis (inflammation of the meninges), where the person has violent headaches, fever and stiff neck muscles, pyaemia (invasion of blood by bacteria) and pneumonia (inflammation of the lungs)?

In serious life-threatening situations there is no doubt in my mind that people should take the pharmaceuticals a doctor is prescribing or undergo a necessary operation. In some instances drugs are lifesavers. This possibility distinguishes us from animals. In nature, many animals die of unresolved conflicts or healing crises.

For many people death is a frightening process. Therefore we have created a life where we attach great importance to developing pharmaceutical drugs that facilitate life and, even in some cases, prolong it. Already as infants, children are injected with vaccines so they become immune and can avoid diseases. As I said before, it is of course a gift to be able to save lives, but the gift also has a reverse side to it. As humans we are potential power, and the only way for us to be able to experience our power is to go through resistance to develop it. It can be likened with fuel, which is potential energy. However it is only when the energy has gone through a carburettor, whereby it goes through resistance, that the force can be extracted.

This process can also be likened with a muscle that we need to exercise by offering resistance and breaking it down, so it will grow stronger.

When we have our children vaccinated, we are unconsciously saying to their systems that they cannot protect themselves against outside interference. However, child disease is nature's way of seeing to it that we receive enough of the resistance we need to be able to build our own defence, which will give us a stronger health in the future. Nature also has its own way of building a defence in children. Mothers transfer anti-bodies for measles to their children, which normally will remain active in the child's body for four years. Breast milk contains TB bacteria, which are not harmful for the child but, on the contrary, creates resistance. Also, during their first years children learn to make contact with the outer world. Conflicts are part of learning to relate to other people and situations. This makes them able to experience child diseases, symptoms in the Regeneration Phase.

How Drugs Work
There are two major functions of a drug. Either it activates the sympathetic nervous system (stressing the organism to a Conflict Phase) or it activates the parasympathetic nervous system (making the organism relax). If we understand the principles we can support healing. It is important to know where we are in the process when the situation has been stabilised, and what we can do to help a person create a Bio–Psycho–Social health.

This Activates the Sympathetic Nervous System (Stressing the Body):

Example: Radiation, cytotoxic drugs (any drugs that damage or destroy cells), cortisone, antibiotics, antihistamines, noradrenalin, caffeine, guaraná (a stimulant that prevents tiredness, headaches and the build-up of lactic acids in the muscles, stays in the organism for about six hours), coca-cola.

Many see a doctor for symptoms belonging to the Regeneration Phase. Example: infections, inflammations, headaches. What pharmaceutical drugs do is stress the body from the Regeneration Phase (active parasympathetic nervous system) so that it activates the sympathetic nervous system. This means that a patient will return to the Conflict Phase where the symptoms normally are non-existent. The pharmaceutical drugs reduce infections, inflammations, headaches, swelling and pain in the Regeneration Phase. When we stop taking the drugs and the disease process is still active the process starts again, and eventually we will be back in the Regeneration Phase, where the symptoms return.

Cortisone is often used to treat itching red eczema, which makes the organism return to the Conflict Phase where the skin is whiter, colder and more insensitive. It we do not rub cortisone on the spot regularly the reddening eczema will return.

This Activates the Parasympathetic Nervous System (Relaxing the Body):

Example: Valium (used for anxiety disorders, to treat agitation, shakiness and hallucinations), morphine (painkiller), lavender, meditation and energy healing.

Severe pain and exhaustion are commonly agreed characteristics for cancer patients in their terminal phase. These pains are actually regeneration signs and unfortunately medical doctors as a rule in the Western developed world, administer morphine doses that can be lethal because they make the patient sink too deeply into the relaxation phase (parasympathetic nervous system). The consequence of morphine is also that the patient becomes more sensitive to pain as the drug leaves the body.

In some cases pain can be seen as something positive, for example when it makes us realise that something is not in balance in our body. In that case the pain is a reminder that there is something that we have to take care of. In other cases it is possible to establish that somebody is in the Regeneration Phase.

Case Study:
My own father went into a strong Regeneration Phase after having seen a reflexologist for a problem he had. His hip hurt so much that he was unable to walk. The same morning he called me and told me that it was the strongest pain he had ever experienced. I told him "Good! Now you know that the hips are healing quickly, exactly as a bone is healing directly after it has been broken." Knowing this, he decided to stay in bed and rest until he got better, while not taking any painkillers. The process took three days. In the morning of the fourth day he woke up and the pain had decreased on his subjective scale from 100 to 1.

Pain is a subjective experience. Watching a comedy or focusing on something funny is a great way of forgetting the pain for a while. Alternative therapists also offer alleviation of pain in the form of acupuncture, reflexology, healing and massage.

The book The *Mozart Effect* tells the story of a trial that was conducted at the St. Agnes' Hospital in Baltimore. Patients from the intensive care unit were offered the opportunity to listen to music by Mozart for 30 minutes. The remarkable thing was that only by listening to the music did they obtain the same results in pain reduction as 10 mg of valium would have done!

If we are talking about a short disease process, pharmaceutical drugs are seldom needed since the body can handle the situation without complications. The most critical moments take place in the Regeneration Phase for some disease programmes like the healing crises for right and left heart attack, pneumonia and liver crises. These crises still have a high mortality rate. Doctors today do their best to help patients through those symptoms.

When is Surgery a Good Idea?

I'm not a medical doctor and what is now going to be

discussed is a view I have received from Dr. Anton Bader, a medical doctor and vice president of the META-Health association.

Many tumours and cysts, which today are operated on as a matter of routine, are actually healing tumours belonging to the Regeneration Phase. Examples of these are cysts on the ovaries, testicles and the kidneys. They are not necessary to operate on unless they disturbed the bodily functions, or if the patient (because of emotional reasons) is unwilling to keep them. Again, it is possible to calculate the time period and intensity of the Conflict Phase to be able to predict how big the tumour is going to grow in the Conflict Phase. If the cyst is small and located in the intestine, the TB bacteria will take it over and destroy it. If the tumour has grown too big, thereby preventing the intestines from working, an operation is usually an option. It is important to carefully discuss the process with the patient, and then let the patient decide if they wanted to have the operation or not.

When it comes to cysts on the ovaries and the kidneys, it is good to wait nine months until they were fully grown. They will grow for as long as a pregnancy. During that time they have no artery and vein system of their own, so they live in symbiosis with another organ that supplies them with blood. If an operation is performed too early, the organ hosting the cyst will be affected. If the patient so desires, or if the cyst is dysfunctional, it can be easily removed after nine months when it will be encapsulated.

8.
Spirit – Bio-Psycho-Spiritual-Social Health through Knowledge and Awareness

This section will complete the knowledge of META-Health and describe a way of life that makes it easier to stay healthy and full of vitality.

The choice to live in conscious awareness and to be willing to take responsibility for ourselves and our lives, is an efficient way of getting along without serious diseases. As human beings we have feelings (Thank goodness, otherwise we would be robots) and unexpected events in our daily lives can make us react strongly. If we pay attention to how we react to what is going on around us, we can release our feelings so that the symptoms will not grow so strong in our bodies.

What health is to you is something you need to define. For me, health means 100% complete spirit (approximate translation from Swedish), which is a state where we have gone beyond the mere absence of physical complaints. It means to be complete on all levels: body, emotions, mind and spirit. I could say that it is let go of who I think I am and awaken more and more to the true Self, which is part of all that is.

In order to explain what I mean by becoming part of all that is, I will refer to the beginning of the section of Disease as a Process, page 28. There I wrote that nature is a symphony of opposites where one does not mean anything without the other. For example: Man–woman, active–passive off-on. None of these could know what they are without each other. You could say that the gift for a man is woman (or visa-versa) because 'she' gives him existence by showing him what is 'isn't and therefore causing existence on that level. We are given the possibility of waking up our entire being by activating and accepting all opposites and aspects of life, nature and the cosmos. In that symphony we are playing our part in harmony with the fantastic orchestra of the universe. We as individuals become one with the universe.

If we are willing to live a life in conscious awareness, it can be really uplifting to learn about some universal laws that help us use our lives as our teacher. They are simple processes that will enable us to become more true to our Self each day, let our body heal plus stay healthy and vital.

Our Map of the World is Creating Our Reality

Let us reconnect with the section "Subjective Experience" from Principle 3, on page 27. Then I talked about that our unconscious interpretation, at the moment of the conflict shock, is a direct reflection of what we already consider true in our inner world. Let's go further into the reasoning.

The human nervous system was created with the purpose of making order out of chaos. And chaos is what we could call the 2.3 million information bits that come rushing towards us every second of our lives. The order we create out of that consists of the thoughts or patterns that we create when we delete, generalise and distort information through our filters. (See picture)

Human Communication Model

Our filters are in fact a collection of memories and experiences, in other words "our inner map". The problem is that none of these memories are real or true. They are nothing but the result of our filtration through our senses and filters, or our "inner map". This is a subjective interpretation or inner representation of what has actually happened.

We could be led to believe that everything we are experiencing through our senses is objective data. Or that what we are experiencing is true. That is not the case though. If the police were to question ten different witnesses about an accident, they would get ten different interpretations on the course of events. Some of the witnesses could even contradict each other. But to the witnesses, these statements would definitely be true.

The problem with the filtration is not that we have a memory. A memory is nothing less than a "captured" present moment to which we have attached a certain importance. If we didn't have a memory we would not be able to know who we are. Problems or conflicts appear only when our memories prevent us from being free and true to our Self. If we have memories telling us that we are successful, then we will have positive thoughts, feelings and body language, creating a behaviour that will help us make new successful decisions. If, on the other hand, we have memories telling us that we are a loser then they will lead us to think limiting thoughts, feel negative feelings and acquire a body language that communicates it making us act in a way that will not lead us to success.

Both scenarios are true, presupposing that a person repeatedly gets evidence of their thoughts, and that one scenario leads to a positive spiral and the other to a negative spiral. (The picture on previous side shows that thought-feeling leads the body chemistry which in turn guides the body language = a behaviour leading to a result).

We have the choice to let go of the truths we have formed in earlier memories. If we were to live in the present moment we would just observe what is happening and live with the truth that every moment has in itself, which is pure potential. Meaning it would either be completely meaningless or have the possibility of containing meaning.

What I actually do when I work with groups or individuals is to have them revisit their memories, consciously or unconsciously, in order to release them so that they once again can be pure potential. This means that they are free to live in the present moment again. The process of releasing memories offers people the possibility of having more options when they interpret and experience a similar situation in the future. If we have the option to choose in a certain situation, very few people would choose to make an experience a negative one.

Think about an experience that used to give you negative feelings. Something happened and you received an insight that made the old meaning and the old memory change. Everybody has had such an experience at some time.

I will give you an example from my own life. In the ninth grade, I went to the school cabaret where my classmates had been working on a show made up of sketches illustrating the school year that had just ended. Suddenly I was witnessing a sketch were my classmates depicted me as a stupid blonde. My own self-image was that I was smart and my image did not change. I decided there and then that no one would ever have reason to think that I was a stupid blonde again. And from that day on I became very serious. In the first meeting with someone I had not met before, I quickly showed them that I had a working mind. Because of that decision there was really no space left for fun and laughter around other people. Until one day when I was taking part in a training session. During the session I could see that the trainer was acting. He interpreted a kangaroo, a dolphin and a strip-tease dancer. But whatever he was interpreting, I could always see who he really was. That insight made me relax and allow myself to have fun again.

Life Is Our Mirror

The phenomenon that life is a reflection of us can be explained with the help of quantum physics. Danish physician Niels Bohr made a groundbreaking discovery (which he later regretted) since it opened up a whole new world for us.

It was presumed at the time that if Bohr could establish that light was either a particle or a wave movement, we would know all there is to know in science.

When he could establish that light was a particle Bohr and others were satisfied. However, until they had completed the whole of the experiment they could not tell if this was true. In the other part of the experiment they found that light also can be a wave movement.

Here's what he said: *"This crucial point...implies the impossibility of any sharp separation between the behaviour of atomic objects and the interaction with the measuring instruments which serve to define the conditions under which the phenomena appear.... Consequently, evidence obtained under different experimental conditions cannot be comprehended within a single picture, but must be regarded as complementary in the sense that only the totality of the phenomena exhausts the possible information about the objects."*

In other words, the measuring equipment will always have a bearing on the result! The presupposition of this experiment leads to a new philosophy of thinking that is still here today. Your mind is a kind of 'measuring equipment'. What you experiment for with this mind, you will find!

The Meaning of Intention

The reasoning shows that if you have the intention or focus on staying healthy, you will find evidence to prove it. If health is important to you, you will unconsciously start catching healthy bits of information from the information stream that every moment sweeps over us in our surroundings. You might notice the positive people at a party, whereas somebody who focuses on problems only notices what is not positive at the same party.

If you are also aware of the principles of META-Health you will have all the odds on your side. All symptoms in the Regeneration Phase are a healthy feedback to you that you have solved a conflict in your life and that your body is about to re-create balance. Knowing this makes it easier for you to have positive feelings in your body, thus accelerating the healing process.

Quantum physics further explains that we are living in an immense sea of energy that reacts on our thoughts. Our thoughts conduct themselves as waves until we identify with them. Before our thoughts develop there is only pure potential. When we identify with our thoughts they start acting as particles. They are born into this world in the form of neuro peptides – matter. The more thoughts, or energy, in the form of feelings we add, the more manifestation there is. Therefore we are able to draw to us the results we wish, or the results we do not wish.

The Law of Attraction

We experience our body and all other matter as solid. If we were to take a closer look at our body under a microscope, we would find that we consist of molecules, which consist of atoms, which consist of a nucleus (neurons and protons) with circulating electrons around. The atom consists mostly of oxygen, thus both we and every other matter consist mostly of oxygen. What makes us experience ourselves as solid is that the atoms are vibrating and thus creating the illusion of being solid. We could be described as vibrating bundles of energy. The Law of Attraction says that "we attract what we are focusing on", which means that we attract the same kind of energy into our lives as what we already have there or need.

In short, this law is about how we act and what we attract. If we are happy we will attract happy events or people into our lives. Conversely if we are worried we will attract worried people or situations to worry about, that is, events that match our vibrations. This phenomenon is described fully in the excellent book *Ask and you will receive by* Ester and Jerry Hicks. The book describes how the Law of Attraction works, and how you can use this knowledge to create your life the way you want it to become.

The focus of releasing old patterns and taking new actions will help you increase your vibration, so that you will be able to experience the health you desire in the future. At the very least, you will have more consciousness about what you are attracting into your life and why.

Imagine your inner map is a magnet attracting to you everything that matches it. If there is something that you are trying to hide in yourself, something you are perhaps unaware of, like a suppressed negative feeling (anger) or a chosen truth (something that you really believe in, like you are not good enough); you will attract people or situations matching your thoughts about the world and life. People you do not like are just there to push the buttons to show you what it is you do not like about yourself. If you wish to stop attracting these people or situations into your life, the solution is to deal with the issue and learn from it - then you will attract them no more.

There is an experiment illustrating how people unconsciously pick up on our filters. In a huge fashion store in England, an experiment was conducted with former pick-pockets who were each put alone in a room to study a film from a certain security camera in the store. They were each asked to choose which customers they would steal from. Believe it or not, they all chose the same victims. The chosen victims would probably be completely unaware of why they were chosen. But if we had the ability to look at the filters of these victims and what they have chosen to believe about the world, we would no doubt find truths like "the world is not a safe place" or "you cannot trust people". A person with this kind of truth on their radar would see incidents involving assaults, robberies, car accidents and the like.

A good friend of mine always used to attract strange men whom she could not trust. When I later learned that her father had sold everything the family owned and left them penniless and with nowhere to live, I understood the connection. This happened when she was only a year old, but it had (on an unconscious plane) influenced the way she related to men, and what kind of men she kept attracting into her life.

This means that there really are no disturbing people or situations around us – only teachers! And when we become aware of that we ourselves are creating our own reality, we can easily change it by changing our thinking and feelings.

I have hundreds of examples of how we are creating our own reality through my own experience and through the stories of the people I have coached and trained. Naturally it is much easier to blame others, but the consequences will then be that nothing really changes.

The moment we become aware of our unconscious patterns or behaviour we will no longer become victims. If we realise what it is we have to learn, we will never react in the same way to a person or a situation again. But if we do not realise what we need to learn, we will attract similar situations time and time again, until we learn and understand the teaching that is there for us.

People opting to stand on the responsibility side and learn about themselves pose questions like:
"Why am I creating this situation over and over again?
"What is it that I am reacting to in this person/situation?"
"How is this situation a reflection on me?"
"What can I learn from this situation?"

9.
The Process to assist a Soulution

The great concepts of the biological principles are laws of our physical reality (The third dimension). The law about the two phases is a law that says that the Regeneration Phase will be as long and as intense as the Conflict Phase, but that is a bit limiting, isn't it?

If people had to experience the pain of the Regeneration Phase if it went on as long as the Conflict Phase, how many people would be excited to do some change in their life? People who fully believed in that concept and didn't have any knowledge about emotional release processes, then they would unconsciously block out any chance to change their negative life situations. This is because if they took the action to do so, their body knows that the regeneration would be very hard and in some cases could lead to death.

So this model I am working from now and that I will share with you is fully focused to release what has caused a symptom, but also reconnect to universal aspects and take new conscious action to actively manifesting new results/situations in our lives.

What I am going to share is consciousness that can assist your current healing potential and whatever healing modality you currently use.

Firstly find the pattern(s) underlying the symptom.
1. Collect the info:
• What is the organ the symptom belongs to?
• What is the conflict that starts the program in that organ?
• If the organ or tissue exists in the whole body, what is the metaphor of the part of the body you have the symptom

in?
- Are you right or left dominant? Do the clap test.
- Does the symptom belong to the Conflict or the Regeneration Phase?

Secondly, release the emotions/patterns with the help of any power technique (E.g. NLP, Time Based Techniques, EFT, TFT, The Journey, TAT, Emotrance, Hypnosis, Deep healing work....). The pattern can be from this life, birth, from the time in the womb, or past down from our ancestors.

Thirdly, when the emotion is released, then the conflict mass of the conflict phase is gone. What is now present? There is now space for the higher learnings; the learnings that are about re-connecting to universal resources the old problem blocked out. When the learnings are present, then there is more freedom to react differently to situations similar to the old problem.

Fourthly, it is about moving forth. What can the person now be, do and have in life? To fully embody the release and to go through a full Soulution, means we also see new results in life. That could be meeting a partner that the old worthlessness pattern stopped us from. It could be to express our gifts by growing our company, instead of the old feeling powerless pattern.

Ask yourself: What am I now inspired to manifest in my life? What actions can I now take; actions that the old issue stopped me from doing? This inspiration comes from the core of your heart. What makes you heart sing?

Example
A boss becomes threatened of a new, younger and intelligent employee and reacts with 'Fear of losing the position'. If he didn't know about surrendering to that reaction, then he would be very stressed for as long as the person is perceived as a threat to his position. One resolution could be that the threat is getting head hunted by another company or that the boss is getting promoted. The fear of losing his position will start a disease process

in the coronary arteries. The artery walls will react with cell minus so they get thinner and can therefore flow more blood through. More blood flow means more strength to fight for the position. In the Regeneration Phase the wall in the coronary arteries wall create cell plus to restore itself. There will also be swelling, and if the cell plus and the swelling is too much, then it leads to a heart attack. As we know, a conflict that would have been going on for more than about 6-9 months, would lead to a heart attack difficult to survive in the healing peak.

When we use tools to release the emotional upset, it means the conflict mass is released from the conflict phase, released from the cellular memory. The conflict mass is equal the conflict length multiplied with the conflict intensity. Releasing the conflict mass is affecting the Regeneration Phase. Often it is healing much quicker and with fewer symptoms. How do we know there has been an emotional release? Before we did the release we could think about an event and feel a strong negative reaction. After the release we can visit the same event and the old negative reaction isn't there any longer.

Releasing a negative pattern may not just be releasing one emotion. A pattern can have 2-10+ aspects, like a real octopus. It can be past life, downloaded from ancestors, from the time in the womb or present life. I have to say that my own stuff and the clients I see rarely have root cases in the present life. How do we notice the pattern is released? My sign is when I/the client are calm, light and expanded for about 3 minutes. If the pattern isn't solved, a new, trapped emotion will come up on the surface before 3 minutes has passed. Sometimes a complex pattern takes more than one session to release all aspects. The body and the unconscious mind know what the next best aspect is to release.

Now if the boss noticed his reaction when the new employee came into his office, and also had awareness about the possibility of letting go of his reaction; then he could chose to see someone who assists him in releasing the fear of losing his position. After the release he could now feel calm, peace and light in the same situation.

When the emotional tension is released you can ask yourself or the client, "What is the learning? What resources have you now got access to that you didn't have just some moments ago? How is this situation perfect? When that learning is coming through, the heart opens and we get re-connected to the universal resources. The learning in his case was that "It is time to move on". He had given what he could give to the company and the profit increased. Now it is time for new ideas to come in for the company to keep expanding, and it is time for him to move on.

If we continue the therapy process with the man and asked what is he really inspired to do instead of working in the company? He shares that for some time he has been inspired by his dream. He would like to set up a B&B, work from home and spend more time in his beloved garden; and serve eco-food for all the guests.

The inspiration, which is a highly intense state in the present moment, meaning we contact with our Spirit and our Self with a big S. That energetic state changes our vibration in our physical body. This is the start to be able to manifest new situations in our physical reality.

The question is how we can assist bringing the inspiration we have into our physical existence? The physical plane is much denser than the higher planes. It is easier to be in the inspiration, than actualize it in our physical world.

The inspiration would contain the new life circumstance that the old pattern blocked. Taking action to bring that into reality is also an action of healing our physical body.

Now, I am not just talking about linear action. A linear action for the man would be to decorate his house, setting up his own business, marketing his B&B service and so on.

However, he can also take energetic actions.

What is an energetic action?

It is a conscious action, which is aligned with the energy that the goal represents for you.

So let's say creating a B&B has the energetic essence of being true to himself. What energetic action could he take?

First of all it is important that it is an action that a person has never taken before. In his case it would have the flavor of being true to himself.

We have to think laterally here, side-stepping a bit.

He could decide to start eating at times when he is hungry, and what his body would truly like to eat in that moment. Before he perhaps ate breakfast before work without being hungry or eating a business lunch when he wasn't hungry.

Taking conscious action is equal to creating a vibrational match for what we like to manifest. Then it is easier to get our dream to come true as well as getting our health back.

After a META-Health course, a woman started to detox her life: Detoxing the body, detoxing her group of friends, detoxing her work. She first noticed the result when she changed shoe size, due to less water retention. It went down one size!

It is not just to think and feel it. Some people get too good at just feeling it, as they were there, but nothing manifests. Then they are still not in a vibrational match here in the physical world to what they would like to create. The easiest way to bring it into the physical is to take new energetic actions, actions that are aligned with the essence of what your inspiration represents.

Alignment of our physical, emotional, mental and higher Self gives us more power to co-create. But in the end, who are we that thinks we are the do-er? Where did the inspiration come from? Life, divine, the One is creating through our physical form to experience different experiences, and ultimately so mystery can experience itself.

10.
An in-depth look at Meta-Health. Survey of the Brain Layers

(Take this journey with caution – this section is going to test your concentration!)

To make sense of this advanced section it's good to remember that we do not have just have one program; we have many systems operating simultaneously. Some of our programs are dated back to the beginning of human kind. Even what we call our brain is made of four separate layers, trying to work as one. These four layers are made up of: The Brain Stem (the earliest human brain, animal-man), The Cerebellum, The Cerebral Medulla and The Cerebral Cortex (man-animal).

It's an exciting time to be alive! Yes, it can be challenging at times, but with consciousness even the challenges are interesting. An important evolutionary shift is happening.

Right now, on a collective level, we are not yet fully humans. We operate as a man-animal, meaning most of us are still reactive beings. We react at other people and situations outside ourselves, with or without consciousness that every reaction is a mirror of our inner world.

For every reaction we heal, we activate the new part of the brain, the frontal lobe. The frontal lobe is linked with the 3rd eye. That activation means we are getting more and more the ability to see the situation as it is, and act in a way that supports the individual, the relationship, the situation and the whole.

Having a quick look at the different brain layers, what are the conflict themes?
Brain Stem - Survival

Cerebellum - Protection
Cerebral Medulla - Self-Evaluation/Devaluation
Cerebral Cortex - Territory/Mental/Social issues

If we saw through those reactions and healed our "inner animal", how would life be? Contemplating that question is helping us to start sensing how life as a human would be like.

For me Meta-Health for is not just about understanding and healing different symptoms. It is about evolving in order to live life expressing your true Self! By recognizing the old patterns (could be the ones the body shows) and heal one after one is a way to let your Self-blossom!

The Brain Stem (BS)

Evolution:
A monad (single cell organism), is directly in contact with and dependent upon its environment (ocean).

Organs Governed by the Brain Stem:
Mouth, thyroid, tonsils, stomach, duodenum, small intestine, appendix, large intestine, rectum, mid-ear, iris, gums, kidney collective tubles, lung alveoli, liver, pancreas, uterus, penis and prostate.

Function:
A life situation associated with survival, ingestion, food processing and reproduction.

Conflicts Originated from the Organs of the Brain Stem:
In the organs of the Brain Stem all conflicts are related to fear of death and digestion. It could be a situation that is too big to be swallowed or digested, like the inability to get hold of, accept, destroy or let go of a situation, or metaphorically, a chunk.

Learning Lesson:

To learn to survive, take care of an individual, a family or a species.

Example of Conflicts:
The Prostate
A man in the UK was experiencing the symptoms of an enlarged prostate. He asked me which conflict was the cause of that. I told him that the conflict had to do with a feeling that he was not man enough. After I had said that, it occurred to him that it was exactly the process he had just gone through. Two months earlier his girlfriend had suddenly announced that she wanted to move out and live by herself. This process had taken two months and they had just solved the situation when I met them, and they had just decided to get married.

In the Conflict Phase there is cell growth causing the prostate to enlarge which will enable the man to produce more secretion and sperm. An enlarged prostate pushes against the urethra, which is why he often feels he needs to use the lavatory more often.

The Cerebellum (Cb)

Evolution:
New functions and organs are necessary. Hormone producing glands (reproduction), nerves, blood and lymph vessels (emulating ocean water, function), bones, tendons (freedom of movement).

Organs Governed by the Cerebellum:
The breast glands, the inner skin layer = the dermis, the pericardium, pleura and the peritoneum.

Function:
A life situation connected with co-ordination, movement, individuality and adaptation.

Conflicts in the Cerebellum:

Conflicts governed by the Cerebellum are related to real or conceived attacks upon the stomach, lungs and the heart, such as a soon to be performed operation or conflicts based on worry and argument.

Learning Lessons:
To define and live by an individual's own integrity and individuality

Example of Conflicts:

Acne
When I started using make-up it became something of a problem to be unmade-up. I didn't feel as beautiful and the feeling changed my personality. When I was wearing make-up I felt more powerful and self-assured. Without make-up I felt insecure and wanted to go and hide myself. After having had fine skin in my early teens, at the age of 18 my skin became a problem. At the same time I became obsessed with the idea that I should lose weight and I generally felt unhappy about myself.

I began taking a contraception pill that helps the skin, and during the next three years my skin was fine. When I stopped taking the pills the acne came back. Actually I had only hidden the problem, which medication often does. By now I was 25 and I knew about META-Health.

The conflict behind acne is to feel deformed or insulted and one has thoughts akin to "somebody is throwing dirt at me". When I understood this it dawned on me that it was I who had insulted myself as I was watching my unmade-up face in the mirror every morning. In the Conflict Phase the dermis is made stronger, which means there is cell growth in order for us to be able to defend ourselves against an attack. In the face, the symptoms appear in the form of blackheads and acne.

Solving this conflict was for a long time a mystery to me. I reasoned that it must have been a physical problem that

I had no power over. It was evident that as a blonde I didn't look as colourful without make-up. That is why I was overwhelmed the day it occurred to me that I didn't look at myself in the mirror in the mornings. I was looking at the energy of my ugly, insulting thoughts. Normally, when I am absorbed by a situation and feel happy, which is a large part of me, I beam and radiate. It then occurred to me that the words "ugly" and "beautiful" are values that are non-existent on the physical plane and that we are all beautiful when we beam and are happy with ourselves and our lives. That is very attractive. Realising this, it didn't take long before my skin got better again.

In the Regeneration Phase the symptom is inflamed acne. If the conflict has been strong it can show up as Tuberculosis of the skin, something that can smell badly.

Breast Cancer

There are two types of breast cancer, lobular (belongs to the Cerebellum) and ductal (belongs to the Cerebral Cortex).

The word lobular stands for cancer (cell growth) in the milk gland. It is caused by a worry or argument conflict. In the Conflict Phase there is cell growth of milk gland cells.

The biological purpose is this: If somebody needs my tenderness and care more milk is produced to give the "nutrition" in the situation. It is a completely normal process during a pregnancy.

Regeneration Phase: The tumour is destroyed with the help of mycobacteria. There is pain, swelling and odour.

The Cerebral Medulla (CM)

Evolution:

New functions and organs are necessary: Hormone producing glands (reproduction), nerves, blood and lymph vessels (emulating ocean water, functions), bones and tendons (freedom of movement).

Organs Governed by the Cerebral Medulla:
Collagen, fatty tissue, cartilage, bones, dental bones, the lymphatic system and lymphatic nodes, blood vessels, arteries and veins, muscles, ovaries, testicles, adrenal cortex.

Function:
A life situation connected with coordination, movement, individuality and adaptation.

Conflicts Governed by the Cerebral Medulla:
These conflicts are all related to problems having to do with self-devaluation (not being good enough) and self-worth, or loss, overwhelming conflicts, or conflicts associated with the water element, for instance a drowning accident.

Learning Lessons:
Define and live an individual's own integrity and individuality.

Example of Case Studies:

A Cyst on the Left Ovary

A 55 year-old woman was diagnosed as having a cyst on her left ovary. The conflict shock relating to ovaries is a loss conflict. Her father unexpectedly died in January 2004. During the Conflict Phase there is destruction of the ovary, which she hardly noticed as she was experiencing deep grief and loss after her father's death. At the same time she was worried about how her mother would cope alone. After a year of mourning, the sorrow turned into a deeply felt loss and at the same time she discovered that her mother was coping better than expected on her own (conflict resolve). This made her exhausted and longing for a vacation to rest. She suddenly started having bleedings, which she had not had since she had the menopause. So she went to see a gynaecologist for a check-up and a cyst was discovered on her left ovary. The biological purpose in the Regeneration Phase is to increase oestrogen production so that the woman will look more attractive, which helps her attract someone to compensate for the loss. We really have to think biologically! Some of her colleagues had remarked that she looked younger than her 40-year old colleague. During the Regeneration Phase there will be a cell growth to fill in the "hole" that was created during the Conflict Phase. She had the doctors remove the cyst as they thought it was too big and pushed against other organs.

When a woman is pregnant however, they do not see any problem in the foetus pushing against other organs and tissues which the growing baby really does.

Biological Explanation for Multiple Sclerosis

Physical symptoms can sometimes strengthen and worsen the emotional crisis that has created it, thereby creating a vicious circle. Some forms of multiple sclerosis (probably even amyotrophic lateral sclerosis - ALS) are triggered by a paralysis conflict that arises when one can neither fight nor escape a situation. Let's get back to thinking biologically. How do animals react when they have no possibility of fighting or escaping? They play dead. In humans the nervous system is affected and causing symptoms of paralysis to occur. The affected place in the body depends on the interpretation we made at the moment of conflict leading to the conflict shock. When the body eventually gets paralysed one can easily imagine how this emotional crisis is strengthened which in turn speeds up the disease process.

To be unable to escape or escape in time	Legs
To be unable to hold or push away	Shoulder, arms and hands

I read the Swedish book *Ro utan åror* by Ulla-Karin Lindquist (published by Nordstedt 2004). Ulla-Karin died from ALS (a paralysis disease). In her book she writes that the doctors do not know the reason for this fatal disease, and on page 56 she shares a dream she had.

"I cannot find my way; I search through different rooms…. I've always chased and been chased, like a deer jumping around in the woods. It hides, flees at the utmost suspicion of danger…" She continues. "I have been driven by adrenaline. I have been looking for chaos. Hunger has been my fuel. Escape my companion in my hunt to be good enough. To be acknowledged. I believe the stress has made me sensitive to the disease."

I feel this dream says a lot and I personally believe that we are always intuitively conscious of the reason for our diseases.

The Cerebral Cortex (C)

Evolution:
Individuals interact with environment and others; requires organs for communication and differentiation.

Organs Governed by the Cerebral Cortex:
Cervix, the alpha and beta cells of the pancreas and canals, urinary bladder, renal pelvis, epidermis (outer skin) including nails and hair, eyelids, eye lens, vitreous body, teeth enamel, nose, heart arteries and veins, sinuses, almost all mucus, bronchial asthma, gall bladder, breast ducts, the possibility of smelling, hearing, seeing and the motoric and sense reflexes.

Function:
Life situations connected with sensory perception, communication and social behaviour and interactions.

Conflicts Governed by the Cerebral Cortex:
Conflicts related to the Cerebral Cortex are connected to territory. They can be about not being able to mark or defend one's territory, or not being able to stand up for a sexual identity or being able to manage a separation. They can also be about a fear or a resistance where one feels that one is being discussed.

Learning Lessons:
To define one's own territory, learn to interact with social environment.

Case Study:

Biological Explanation for Passing Kidney Stones
Linda, 40, had just had problems with passing kidney stones, a very painful process, when I met her in the autumn of 2005.

At the end of March 2005 a sudden feeling came over her that her husband was cheating on her again. It made her want to move out. She felt frustrated, unable to sleep between 1:00am and 4:00am and she got hypertension (high blood pressure). All these symptoms are typical of the Conflict Phase where the shock comes from somebody being unable to mark his or her territory.

This kind of conflict relates to the pelvis. What happens biologically is that there is a destruction of the pelvis area during the Conflict Phase, with the purpose of enlarging the area of the pelvis, making it possible for more urine (to mark the territory with) to flow through. Kidney stones are formed and minor pain and spasm can be experienced as a consequence.

In mid-July 2005, she took part in a training course to

become an NLP practitioner, where she practised Time Based Techniques and Hypnosis, among other things. During the course of the training she released negative feelings, and when she came home to her husband they both experienced their relationship as newly born (conflict resolve).

She started feeling exhausted, even though she was at peace with herself and was having a wonderful time with her husband (Regeneration Phase). At the end of July she started feeling pain in her right kidney, and the pain increased until the stones passed through her urethra for four consecutive days. On September 3rd the process was over and she now has normal blood pressure again.

As you can see from above, in the Regeneration Phase the conflict process is reversed. The kidney stones start dislocating in order to be eliminated through the urine and it hurts (the bigger the grain the more it hurts). Inflammation is normal during the Regeneration Phase.

Case Study:

Biological Explanation for Long Sightedness
Woman from Los Angeles, 49, long sighted in both eyes.

The woman had been married to a dominant man for 17 years and in 2002 she started to release herself from his dominance, thus becoming more independent. This was when he hit her for the first time, giving her a black eye. He threatened that if she were to leave him he would kill her (the conflict shock was fear for an unpredictable situation). She quickly became longsighted on her right eye since the conflict had to do with her partner. She discovered that she was unable to read without glasses, whereas she could see well at a distance (Focus on seeing the fear in advance in order to be prepared). He struck her many times, and her sight in the left eye was also affected (many repeated conflicts of the same kind balances the brain and moves the conflict over to the other side of the brain).

During the Conflict Phase there is cell destruction in the retina, with the biological purpose of not wanting the lurking danger to come close.

She finally left her husband at the beginning of April 2005, and had to go into hiding from him with her daughter. As the husband unexpectedly passed away at the end of April 2005, the threat disappeared and the conflict was resolved.

She then entered a Regeneration Phase when her eyesight was first dramatically got worst (due to the swelling, the oedema, on the side of the brain). She was relieved not to have to hide anymore and felt free to fully lead the life she wanted. At the same time she was tired and listless over the summer.

She understood the biological process and the higher purpose of what she had learned from the situation with her husband. She started training Chinese eye-movements, meditating twice a day and planning the business idea she had had for some time. Three months later, when I last heard from her, her eyesight had steadily improved.

Biological Explanation for a Heart Attack
In a conflict involving a fear of losing a territory, the wall of the coronary arteries are reacting with cell destruction. Why is that? The heart must be able to pump more blood to the body. When the conflict is over, the coronary veins return to normal in the healing phase and when they heal there might be swelling or some kind of a scab on a wound that can cause coronary arteries to become clogged. When this conflict is debilitating to the functioning of the system and the blood supply is interrupted, we call it a heart attack (the healing peak).

The risk of a fatal heart attack becomes imminent if the conflict has been active for more than eight months. If the conflict has been going on for a shorter period of time, the heart attack might be felt as a heart flutter only. It is important to say that when a person is going through an emotional release, we have seen evidence of people surviving what they wouldn't have survived if they didn't release the conflict mass of the Conflict Phase. Then the Regeneration Phase becomes safer.

Biological Reason for Congestion
Congestion is a symptom of the Regeneration Phase. The conflict is that something "stinks" or irritates. During the Conflict Phase the mucus in the nose is broken down. When the situation is resolved it is being restored again, which is experienced as swelling, congestion, a runny nose and infection. Bleeding from the nose is a normal symptom.

Biological Reason for Cancer in the Breast Ducts
Cancer in the breast ducts is in the layer of cells that form the walls of the breast glands. It is caused by a separation conflict when, for instance, an individual is being separated from a partner, a child, parents or the nest.

In the Conflict Phase there is cellular destruction in the breast ducts, which causes loss of sensitivity (there is less sensitivity in the nerves inside the ducts), the biological intention being that one is better equipped to cope with the separation, to allow more milk to flow.

In the recovery phase there is cell growth to build up what was lost during the Conflict Phase, which leads to intensive swelling behind the nipple, inflammation, enlargement and hypersensitivity.

11.
Microbes – Biological Helpers

This law will turn what we have learned earlier upside down. The microbes are not the cause of problems, but they are assisting the process during the Regeneration Phase. We can compare this to the example of a child who had witnessed two fires during the same week and firemen working to put out the fire — the child thought it was the firemen who caused the fires because they were always there at a fire!

The brain directs the microbes, which means that the immune system, the way we know it, does not exist. Fungi, bacteria and viruses can only become active after a conflict is resolved in the Regeneration Phase, and when they do they only do so in a specific organ. There are microbes within us constantly and they can be transferred to us from our environment. However, they are inactive as long as we do not go through a regeneration process that has to do with the brain layer concerned by the conflict.

This demonstrates the perfect purpose for the microbes. Previously Principle Number five explained that there is a connection between the diseases related to each layer in the brain. Principle Number six in this section will explain how the microbes belong to each layer in the brain. In the case of a disease related to a certain brain layer, the same group of microbes will be present in the regeneration process.

Brain Stem

BS - Fungi & Micro Bacteria
Example: Tuberculosis & Candida
Fungi and micro bacteria are the oldest microbes there are that are governed by the Brain Stem. Their task is

to destroy tumours in the intestines, lungs and the liver. Fungi and micro bacteria will start increasing the very moment the conflict shock occurs at the same speed as the cells are growing in the organ or the tissue. During the Conflict Phase they are latent and can only be activated in the Regeneration Phase. If there are not enough bacteria to destroy the tumour (if the person has taken antibiotics) the tumour becomes encapsulated and stays that way. Normally the person will have a temperature and nightly sweating when the destruction process is taking place.

Cerebellum

Cb - Fungi & Micro Bacteria
Example: Tuberculosis
The micro bacteria governed by the Cerebellum are called "cleaners" and they only work with organs and tissues governed by this brain layer. They help destroy breast cancer tumours and skin cancer. The bacteria help fill up tissues with scar tissue.

Cerebral Medulla

CM - Bacteria
Example: Streptococci (translation streptos, meaning easily bent, like a twisted chain)
Bacteria governed by the brain marrow will fill up the holes in the bones and restore them. Some of them are also present when restoring ovary and testicle tissue.

Cerebral Cortex

C - Viruses
Example: Hepatitis, herpes, influenza
Viruses are the youngest microbes from an evolutionary perspective. They have been found in organs and tissue governed by the Cortex. They are restorers and fill up

the cell losses that took place under the Conflict Phase. Viruses start growing after the conflict is resolved. The Regeneration Phase, which has to do with viruses, can often become very intense since fever and inflammation also belong to this phase.

Example:
This example shows how illogical it is to say that viruses and bacteria spread.

At the Regeneration Phase of lung cancer there are Tuberculosis bacteria (TB) present, which will help the body destroy the cancer tumour. In the Regeneration Phase of a bronchus cancer there are viruses present to restore the tissues, meaning cell growth, but this phase is often misinterpreted as a dangerous cancer tumour.

Despite the fact that the bodily parts are connected, the TB bacteria do not spread to the bronchi or vice versa. The viruses in the bronchi do not spread to the lung alveoli. The TB bacteria on the other hand, can be found in the intestines where they are destroying the intestinal cancer tumour in the Regeneration Phase. The intestines and the lung are both governed by the Brain Stem, whereas the bronchi belong to the Cortex.

I encourage you to explore the correlation of microbes and symptoms, instead of only seeing them as the causation. Find out what's true for you.

APPENDIX 1
THE UNDERLYING CAUSE OF...

... *Metastases*

The theory of how cancer comes into existence is in principle that a single cell spontaneously, or due to some kind of chromosomal injury, starts dividing rapidly and grows into a life-threatening tumour. According to traditional Western medicine, the cancer cells furthermore have the capacity of spreading, both by growing into nearby organs and through the blood stream or lymphatic system to the rest of the body.

According to today's treatment principles, quickly growing cancer cells are eliminated by means of operation as quickly as possible. Patients can recover that way, but it happens that cancer develops in other parts of the body, and these cancer cells are then called daughter cells or metastases.

Lothar Hirneise, Europe's leading cancer specialist, is working for the National Foundation for Alternative Medicine in Washington. He has written the book *Chemotherapy heals Cancer and the World is flat*. In the book he discusses some contradictions to the theory that cancer would spread.

• Why is it that our heart is never stricken by cancer? The heart also consists of billions of cells, which do not seem to mutate and become cancer cells.
• Most metastases grow in the liver, lungs, head or skeleton. If cancer spreads, why is it that a tumour never starts in the little finger, the spleen or the kidneys?

The Swedish Cancer Foundation (Cancerfonden) website says that breast cells have been found in the lungs as daughter tumours. Normally every kind of tissue produces different kinds of tumours. Today the theory of metastases is based on assumptions and hypotheses. Convincing evidence on what they based their assumptions on is still lacking today, according to Hirneise.

Below I will take an interesting experiment from page 68 of the book *Chemotherapy Heals Cancer and the World is Flat* by Lothar Hirneise. *McKinney exchanged a cell nucleus from a leopard frog for a malign nucleus from a cancer cell. After fertilisation completely healthy frogs were born. Genes have been said to be responsible for a person developing cancer or not, but in this instance when a healthy cell nucleus was exchanged for a cancer nucleus, nothing happened!*

Could the reason for metastases be that the person comes into another conflict? I would say so, because a biological disease program must be activated by a conflict shock for cells to be able to grow in the first place. Otherwise, not even transplanted cancer genes can cause a growing tumour.

Case Study:
Let me give you another example. A lady came to the hospital and was diagnosed with breast cancer. A CT-scan was taken showing circular formations on the part of the brain that relates to the breast. After the diagnosis another picture was taken and at that time new circular formations were found on the part of the brain that related to the lung, which stands for fear of death. Shocking diagnoses like this and words like cancer which cause apparent fear in people, can lead to further conflicts, which can lead to further types of cancer.

Having a breast removed can have the consequence of the woman reacting with a new conflict:

Example:
"I am not good enough anymore" – a conflict that can lead to bone cancer

"I am less worthy" – conflict that can lead to lymphatic cancer
"Fear of death" – a conflict that can lead to lung cancer

Case study:
A colleague of mine who works with META-Health in Los Angeles told me about an interesting patient case. He had seen a patient with breast cancer who after radiation treatment learned that the cancer had spread to the liver. What the therapist quickly found out was that the woman had invested a lot of money in her cancer treatment. She, in her capacity as a small business owner, had not had the strength to work during the Regeneration Period. Consequently she had become broke. As a result of this, a new conflict shock arouse, this time a hunger conflict. This is when one fears that there is not enough money for food and shelter, which will cause cell growth in the liver.

Case Study:
Another female patient, who had recently taken part in one of my trainings in META-Health, was diagnosed SLE (chronic fibrositis) or possibly even cancer because her blood values were not good. She realised that she was in the Regeneration Phase and that the symptoms were inflammation in the connective tissues. She actually told the doctor that she didn't have cancer, and that he should be careful not even to think so if he wasn't sure of it himself. If she had believed him or reacted with fear of death, the lung alveoli could have started dividing which could have resulted in a real tumour there eventually.

More research is definitely needed when it comes to metastases. It would be very interesting if CT-scans could be part of the standard examination. Then we could say for certain that the patient has experienced yet another conflict shock. Humans and animals react according to the same special program of nature, but the animals seldom develop metastases. Why is that? Could it be that they do not understand diagnoses?

... Cancer of the Brain

After a conflict has been resolved, the earlier hyperactive brain area will react with heavy swelling because superfluous liquid is being squeezed out of the brain. Symptoms of this can be headaches or other symptoms depending on which parts of the brain the swelling pushes against. The swellings are visible on a CT-scan in the form of dark circles, and they can easily be interpreted as a brain tumour. You can see it clearly on the picture below on the right brain half.

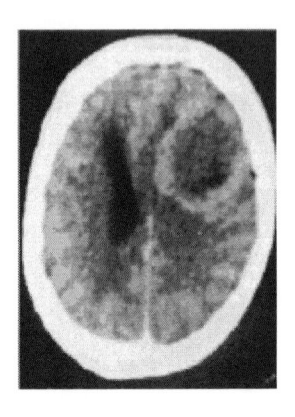

The water accumulation contains glial cells (special connective tissue of the central nervous system, composed of different cells with various supportive and nutritive functions, make up some 40 per cent of the total volume of the brain and spinal cord). These are used to repair the brain tissue and they remain until the tissue has been healed. The condition of the brain is successively normalised, and the result after healing is a strengthened support tissue. This means an increased capacity to handle this kind of conflict in the future. If the conflict has been long and intensive, the symptoms can be life threatening.

It is important to check if there is a kidney collecting tubule conflict active (feeling alone, abandoned). If it is, then the body is holding more water and that makes the swelling bigger. When you release that conflict then the water will release and it can cause the swelling in the brain to get smaller.

If the doctor would find cells from another tissue in the brain tumour, i.e. the lungs, then look for the correlation of the conflict theme that affected the lung.

... Chronic Diseases

Within traditional medicine in the Western developed world, chronic diseases are something that we often identify as incurable diseases. The symptoms will probably be there for the rest of one's life. Within Chinese medicine, on the other hand, chronic symptoms are regarded as a longer healing process. This way of seeing things makes the patient meet with an attitude that implies that healing is possible after all. META-Health will explain the process of chronic symptoms. But first we will have to understand what a trigger is.

... A Trigger

The environment where a person physically was at the moment of a conflict shock is stored as a memory in his or her unconscious mind. It is nature's way of warning us and preparing us for similar dangers in the future. The circumstances around the conflict are linked together at a neurological level, and we call them triggers. When the individual encounters a trigger after a conflict shock it leads the body–brain–mind react in the same way as it did at the moment of the conflict shock. A trigger is what the mind registers at the exact moment of the conflict, or in other words:

- What we saw (Who was with us in the situation, the environment, pictures, dreams etc.)
- The sounds we heard (A specific tone of voice.)
- The prevailing feelings we had during the moment we

experienced the conflict.
• Tastes (What we were eating at the moment the conflict occurred.)
• Smells (The perfume somebody wore.)
• Words (What we said to ourselves at the moment the conflict occurred.)

Many diseases like allergies, migraine, colds, and haemorrhoids come about by means of a trigger being activated. If a conflict shock occurs at the same time a person is eating an orange, this person becomes allergic to oranges. If a person experiences a conflict shock in the spring when there is pollen, around he or she becomes allergic to pollen. If you want to find out the primary cause of your allergy and what it is a trigger for, you need to become observant of the feelings that are linked to that which releases the allergy.

Case Study
A young woman wanted me to help her with her sugar addiction. She had been going in and out of treatment centres during the last six weeks and before we met she had gained 17 kilos as a result of overeating. I immediately thought of her pancreas, which stands for fear–disgust–conflict. During our meeting she revealed to me she had been sexually abused as a child.

When we find ourselves in a situation that we experience as unpleasant, the fight or flight reflex is activated and the body has a surge for quick energy which we get from sugar.

In her case this reflex was triggered each time she thought of the person who had abused her sexually, which made her body crave more sugar. Her unconscious mind was still thinking fight or flight, since the conflict had still not been resolved within her.

If a person is in constant contact with a trigger that activates the conflict, it leads to a negative spiral: In the long run this becomes very exhausting for the body. If for example the job one holds during the daytime is involved in the conflict, the person goes into the Conflict Phase during the daytime and the Regeneration Phase at night.

Probably many of our classical, well-defined diseases are just that, bad circle lapses. Repeated conflicts expose the brain tissue for stress like repeated swelling – non-swelling – tissue growth. In these cases the natural process can result in a serious, chronic disease, or it can turn out to be fatal.

When we understand the importance of finding the trigger and releasing it (emotional work or changing environment), then we will have the possibility to heal chronic diseases.

... Secondary Gains

Another important factor when it comes to chronic diseases is that many individuals feel that they gain more, consciously or unconsciously if they keep their diseases, instead of getting well. There is a term for this, "secondary gain". It might sound completely improbable, but it has proven true. If a person has been ill for some time and this person's life has formed around the disease, it can be frightening to make the changes needed. The disease could even be more important than the individual's own health.

Normal gains are:
- Sympathy from loved ones
- Insurance money
- Husband/wife and children help out in the home
- Social position

Case Study
A lady was seeing a professional therapist and everything went well during their last session until the last bit was to be released. They came to a dead stop. The therapist

asked her why she didn't allow herself to release the last bit? To which she answered that it was nice to see all the therapists in town. Also, it was her husband who was paying for the sessions and she didn't have to work.

...Diseases that are Genetically Inherited

DNA Equals our Feelings
In this section we will take a look at research explaining the reason for genetically inherited diseases. The research is made by the Scientist and Professor of Cellular Biology Dr. Bruce H. Lipton at Stanford University School of Medicine and author of the book *Biology of Belief: Unleashing the Power of Consciousness, Matter and Miracles.*

Before the 15th Century the mission of the scientists was: "To understand the 'Natural Order' so that humanity would be able to live in harmony with it."

After the 15th century Newton and Descartes decided that we did not need God. They thought the universe and the body worked like machines. They thought that we only had to learn how the different parts worked and then exchange those that did not work, thereby solving problems.
"All that Matters is – Matter", they said.

Still today modern science is striving towards developing the knowledge of how the different parts relate and interact with each other so that it can be used to dominate and control nature. From the Newtonian way of seeing things some presuppositions have been developed, e.g. that genes control the biological functions in our bodies.

Our bodies consist of some 60 billion cells and each separate cell contains within itself all the bodily functions there are (the neural system, digestive apparatus, blood system, skeleton etc). The big question has always been: What controls each cell? We have for a long time thought that

DNA would be stable, and thereby could not be changed and that the cell nucleus was a control centre. That theory has originated in the belief that we cannot influence what we have inherited.

What contradicts the theory is, according to Dr. Lipton, the cell nucleus can be extracted and it can continue to live for two more months in a test tube. This means that the presumption of genes governing our biological function is wrong. Genes cannot give themselves a message. They need signals from the outside. The purpose of the cell nucleus is reproduction, and not to control the cell.

If the Cell Nucleus Does Not Govern the Cell, Then What Does?

Dr. Bruce Lipton used a DNA sample from a patient and put it under a microscopic lens on the other side of the room. He then asked the man to think about something that he liked in himself and about something that he disliked. The result of this experiment was that he could observe how the DNA of the man changed at the same moment he thought the different thoughts about himself. Dr. Lipton discovered that the protein in the cell membrane acts as receptors and takes in the chemical substances that are present in the blood stream, and that the substances are constantly changing our genes. The substances are secreted out of the feelings we have at every given moment, something that was also confirmed by Dr. Deepak Chopra, (he wrote about how neuro transmitter supplied the body-mind connection). Thus it is not the genes but our thoughts that create disease. Dr. Lipton proved that our belief system, whether true or false, positive or negative, will influence the genetic activity and in fact our genetic code.

What further confirms his findings is that if we take out the receptors from the cell membrane we will be unable to react at anything at all, thus we will lose behaviours. But if the cell nucleus is taken out, the cell will still live on for a limited period of time.

A lonely cell is able to survive on its own, but it has a greater chance of surviving together with others and when many cells are working they need a leader, our brain.

The work of Dr. Lipton gives humanity hope and it has been regarded as one of the most remarkable findings within the new sciences.

Language gives us, in principle, unlimited possibilities to express ourselves, and even the genetic alphabet gives us options for different choices of words. Our genes do not limit us when it comes to what we can say. What limits us is merely how we interpret the words.

How Diseases Become Inherited

Dr. Bruce Lipton presents a trial with two cloned mice embryos, which were implanted into two separate females. One mouse was put in a stressful environment, and the other in a calm environment. Cloned mice should be born identical, but such was not the case. The mouse, which had been living in a stressful environment, had athletically built offspring with a less developed frontal lobe (part of the brain), indicating a lesser level of intelligence. The genes had been adopted so that the mouse would be able to defend itself in a stressful environment. The offspring born to the mouse in a calm environment did not have as many muscles, but they had a well-developed frontal lobe. Their genes were adapted for intelligence.

The individual's perception of reality, positive or negative, produces different hormones in the bloodstream. The embryo receives this information and its genes adapt accordingly to make the embryo ready to cope with the environment into which it is to be born.

From the moment we are born we will learn from our parents how we are supposed to relate to different situations in life. This means that they can unconsciously transfer their fears to their children, who probably will react in the same way their parents would in the case of an unexpected conflict.

This means that we can develop the same diseases as our parents have had. Note, however, that weak genes only become active in a stressful situation like a conflict shock.

APPENDIX 2
CANCER AND THE SOCIETAL DEVELOPMENT

The top three types of cancers in Sweden (source: www.cancerfonden.se, statistics from 2006)

Females

Per cent	**Number of Cases**	
29.5	6 925	Breast cancer
7.8	1 842	Colon cancer
6.1	1 429	Lung cancer

Males

Per cent	**Number of Cases**	
36.8	9 882	Prostate cancer
7.5	2 028	Skin cancer, excluding malign melanoma
6.7	1 806	Lung cancer

At the top of the list for women there is breast cancer and for men there is prostate cancer. We all seem to know somebody who has been diagnosed with these symptoms. Breast cancer is more than three times as normal as colon cancer on the list for women, and prostate cancer is more than four times as normal as skin cancer, excluding malign melanoma on the list for men.

When we study medical literature we often find no explanation as to why we are stricken with cancer. We only find a number of risk factors like unhealthy food, lack of exercise, stress and genes. The interesting thing is that 70% of those diagnosed with breast cancer or prostate cancer do not relate to the mentioned risk factors at all.

In the 1940's the risk of a woman developing breast

cancer was 5% and in 2005 the American Cancer Society calculated the risk to be as much as 13%. Could it be that billions of kronor in research have not diminished the risk at all? The cost for pharmaceutical drugs for cancer per 1,000 inhabitants in the Uppsala-Örebro region was 213,000 SEK in Sweden in 2005. But still cancer is regarded as the most common cause of death among those younger than 75 years of age.

I would like to discuss what has happened in the Western developed world since the 1940's from a socio-political point of view. After the Second World War women were forced to go out working as they were needed in industry and thus their liberation began. A woman was no longer dependant on a man. The old rule, that the man was the breadwinner and the woman took care of the home and children didn't work anymore. Still today, man and woman are finding new ways to relate to each other. During this development period conflicts have become more common relating to separation and worry/conflict. (A separation conflict lies behind cancer in the breast gland ducts and a worry conflict lies behind cancer in the breast gland). Those conflicts were rather unusual before the 1940's.

Findings of a Finnish Study
Events like divorce, to be made redundant, or the passing away of a family member are associated with a higher risk that those affected by it develop breast cancer. (American journal of Epideriology 2003;157:415-423)

Dr. Kirsi Lillberg et al, University of Helsinki, have investigated the connection between overwhelming events in life and breast cancer. The study included 10,808 women aged 18 and upwards in a Finnish Cohort during the period of 1976–1996. The results showed that no factors based on personality or stress due to daily activities, how happy one was with one's life situation, how extrovert one was, on the risk of breast cancer. Neither did BMI (body mass index), weight changes, alcohol consumption, smoking, or physical activity have any effect on breast cancer. What did, however, was the accumulation of life events together with some single events of major importance. Irrespective of the total events in life it was divorce/separation, the death of a spouse or a near relative or friend that could be associated with a high cancer risk.

Prostate Cancer
Biological Function in the Body:
In the prostate a thin floating liquid is produced which at the moment of semen discharge is mixed with the semen cells. The liquid provides nutrition to the semen cells so that they will be able to swim the long way to fertilise the egg cell. In other words, the liquid makes the male sperm good enough to be fertilised. The growth and function of the prostate is stimulated by the male hormone testosterone.

What often lies behind cell growth (a tumour) in the prostate is a subjectively experienced "ugly" territory conflict. This conflict is often linked to emotional problems or circumstances that are related to the man "not feeling man enough".
A man used to need a strong territorial instinct in the past when it was his duty to protect his woman and his children. There could be as many as 15 children in a family in those days. A man has it in his genes that he needs to have a say. When a woman leaves a man he cannot reproduce, which in the old days meant he was not able to survive. Our biological instincts have not changed much during the last 50 years, even if we drastically have changed our way of living.

Below we will list a number of conflicts that have been reported within the META-Health network, here summarised by Johannes Fisslinger, President and founder of the META-Health network.

• A man discovers that his wife is cheating on him with a younger man.
• During a divorce process "ugly" things come out in the

open.
• A young woman left her husband for a younger, more vital man.
• A farmer was forced to give away his farm to a son against his will.

The Conflict Phase
There is cell growth in the prostate, which enlarges it. Typical symptoms are that the prostate starts pushing against the urinary urethra, which makes the man want to urinate more often. Following a long and intensive conflict a tumour develops.

Biological Purpose
The biological purpose is that the production of the thin flowing liquid increases.

If the man does not resolve the conflict the tumour continues growing. If he resolves the conflict, he goes into the Regeneration Phase. In that case the tumour is either quickly eliminated by the help of TB bacteria or encapsulated if there are not enough of them. Inflammation is a normal complication in the Regeneration Phase.

Cancer in the prostate is most common among men over 70 years of age. According to the Swedish Cancer Foundation, the disease is unusual before the age of 50.

Discussion

In Sweden, like in the rest of Europe and the USA, cancer in the prostate is very common; whereas it is very unusual in countries like China and Japan. The reason could be that men in these countries have not regarded women as a threat against their masculinity. In these countries males have traditionally been those who make decisions and take initiatives and females have been submissive. Today the roles are loosening up in pace with female emancipation and women are taking up more space in society.

Liver Cancer

The occurrence of liver cancer is very unusual as a primary cancer in Sweden. If a person develops liver cancer it is often the case of metastases (a medical doctor in the Western world would say that cancer spreads). On the other hand, liver cancer is a very common kind of cancer on the African continent.

Mozambique - cancer is liver cancer	70%	of	all
Senega - cancer is liver cancer	67%	of	all
Bantu in South Africa - cancer is liver cancer	50%	of	all
India, China, Taiwan, the Philippines - cancer is liver cancer	20%	of	all
USA, Canada, and Western Europe - cancer is liver cancer	2-3%	of	all

(Neumayr, A and Weiss, W: Liver Tumours - New aspects. Hepatogastroenterology 28:1,1981)

Liver Cancer is Caused by a Starvation-Existence Conflict

The biological function of the liver cells is to absorb our nutrition from the food we are digesting. The biological purpose of a cell growth in liver cells after a conflict (which has to do with starvation or existence) is that the liver starts producing more bile. This enables it to absorb more nutrition from the tiny food portion a starving person is getting.

If the conflict is solved the person goes into Regeneration Phase, and TB bacteria break down the tumour. Exhaustion, fever, nightly sweating and cirrhosis of the liver are symptoms in this phase.

Discussion

A starvation conflict is very uncommon in Sweden and in the Western developed World. It is in fact more common in Africa. According to the Swedish Cancer Foundation 374 cases of primary liver cancer were diagnosed in 2003. However, a third of all who are diagnosed with cancer will develop metastases in the liver at some time. That corresponds to 15,000 cases in all.

To make sense of the above statistics, you could look back to the section about metastases (page 104). You could even look at calling metastasis 'secondary cancer'. As a reminder, to go through a cancer process can mean huge changes in one's life. One starts pondering over existential questions. We can look back to the case where a woman developed cancer in the liver after a prolonged treatment period for breast cancer. After having spent a lot of money on her breast cancer treatment, and at the same time running a small business; she did not have the strength to work during her regeneration period, and she ended up broke. Thus, there was a new conflict. This new conflict shock of starvation was not to have enough money for food and shelter. Thus the liver reacted to this new issue.

Post Script

I see META-Health as a natural next step in medicine and health. On the web page of the Swedish Cancer Foundation it says: "We will conquer cancer. Would you like to help us do so?" My answer to the question is: "Yes, I want to help. Not with focus on conquering, but with the intention of teaching people to understand the biological purpose of the disease process, and to help those who want to solve possible ongoing conflicts and create a good environment for healing."

The fact that we are aware of the principles of META-Health will not cause unemployment to physicians, researchers or the pharmaceutical industry, because the people employed in the industry are also needed as part of the disease process. My vision and wish is that traditional Western medicine in the developed world and META-Health will be able to work together with the knowledge of how nature and the body work. We would then be able to create much better prerequisites for healing – both on a physical, emotional, mental and spiritual level. The doctors who will diagnose possess the know-how of how to perform operations or administer medication. A META-Health trained caregiver will explain the disease process to the patient and help create the best prerequisites for the healing process. Naturally the patient's wishes will be governing the process. If he or she wishes to undergo surgery or take a certain kind of pharmaceutical drug even if the situation is not acute, it is important to listen to the patient. The power of the placebo effect is well known to help healing.

All therapies are valuable and could be even more efficient with the knowledge of META-Health. Let us work together and create a network that supports everybody's journey to awareness and health.

About the Author

By Asa Brita Simonsson.

The way I know Susanne is her wisdom and knowledge around conflicts within illnesses. Her playfulness and ease makes everything a lot easier to meet if you happen to be in a middle of a conflict. That playfulness also plays an important role when she is out in the field as a teacher, as she can easily meet all the energies we need to understand...and the vast complexity of it all transforms to a playground. A playground where each and every one of us can choose the toy we want to play with to make it work.
She radiates the light of a Master... and the best of all... she gives you the mirror of it all, and gives you the possibility to awaken your own Master giving you the idea of the purpose to it all. As a result of that, things that seems so vast and complex like illnesses and pain turns into the simplicity and pureness it came from, Pure Life!
Susanne is a Master in the meeting of just that Special Limit... in that so Very Special Own Limit, a brand in itself of importance, as she realize that importance, she meets it with such a big Love and curiosity that the energy of the Limit itself...bursting.... And the power of that makes it transform itself to the source of Love it came from.
In that second happens such a vast respect for Life, that Life

finds its way Home. As a Teacher Susanne has a structured way of teaching and shares her art of wisdom on a very high level, where she methodically journeys through the facts around the subject she teaches. A splendid cocktail of energies in a combination that reflects abundance!

You can have the body and life you are wiling to stand for.
I know that you too can create your life just the way you want it. Everybody can, because everybody is free to choose. The only thing that is very important is to contemplate "Who am I and what am I choosing?" For me it feels like a true choice comes from the One, filtered down through the soul self and higher self, which feels like inspiration in our human body. That inspiration will always be our next step of evolution, and therefore it will feel like it is outside our comfort zone. When we follow that inspiration and the guidance we get step by step, then we are always evolving to live more and more true to our Self. If the ego listens to "you can have what it wants", then other thoughts come along. Thoughts like "It would be nice to win on the lottery so I then can do what I want". Where is the evolution in that desire? It doesn't exist. The evolution would probably be "I like to do what makes my heart sing and earn money from it". Then ask for guidance of what steps we need to take to let that come true.

I can help you understand your own disease and release your emotional blocks and facilitate Soulutions. You can book a private session with me or take a training course in META-Health conducted by me. I will help you understand your symptoms so that you can heal yourself.

In Sweden, medical doctors diagnose and decide upon which treatments to give their patients, especially when it comes to cancer and diabetes. I look forward to working alongside doctors applying a META perspective and using an integrative medicine plan in the treatment of patients.

Training in META-Health

This is the training course for all those who are interested in their own health and for those who are making a living helping other people with their health. The training course will make you certified according to the International META-Health standard (IMMA), step 1.

The META-Health principles are introduced. This is coupled with breakthrough information and insight given exercises, which guaranteed transform your way of thinking when it comes to health and disease. It will also become clear to you how you can use this kind of information to help yourself, your loved ones and possible clients.
On the www.metamedicine.se website you can find our more about the training and take part of the on-line training at anytime. You can also arrange META-Health training in your town and I will run it there.

Testimonials

I have received a much deeper understanding of how the body and "diseases" work and how they are living together in symbiosis, all according to nature's way of solving "problems".
Stefan Johansson, NLP-coach, Sandviken

META-Health has finally given Chinese medicine and the whole alternative care an acknowledgement. It builds upon the same basis and can, be measured, proven and accepted. META-Health is here to stay and it will be an eye-opener. Those who earlier did not want to see cannot close their eyes anymore for what is evident and obvious.
Ylva Brygg, Qi gong therapist, Östersund

I was introduced to the principles of META-Health by, Terry Elston, the founder of NLP World. Within a few hours, my concepts of why people become ill and how they can heal were changed around. After years of working in the medical profession, all the pieces started to come together of why emotions can trigger illnesses. Far from being another nebulous holistic concept, META-Health was founded by a German doctor who has meticulously provided the radiological and histological evidence for the system. The result is nothing short of a revolution for science and medicine providing a quantum leap forward in integrated health paradigms.

Susanne Billander is a superb trainer, who not only provides the intellectual framework for this system, but also conveys a deep sense of holism and unity that goes beyond words. I thoroughly recommend this course.
Dr Manjir Samanta-Laughton, MBBS, GP and author of Punk Science

When the concept of META-Health was presented to me I discovered what I for a long time, had already suspected

but not had the words or substance for. It is the glue that binds everything together. My understanding of how we function became complete. META-Health is a real Eureka-experience from beginning to end!
Catharina Westerberg, nurse, Reflexology therapist and Coach

The META-training was really an eye-opener for me and as such a very powerful one. Susanne is a great teacher and very clear when she presents the whole thing. Also, she is full of passion for the subject.
Emma – Louise Wilson, Driver NLP to empower, Cambridge

Thank you Susanne. This was my life assurance. When one understands how the body works in a biological way the fear of a disease suddenly striking vanishes.
Sebastian Amenta, Siracusa

I got a deep understanding of what is happening in my own body – I'd like to express it like this: I came nearer to my own body. What before was mysterious became completely logical. Curiously I now ask myself: What is the reason for this symptom? Instead of, bad luck that I was affected.
Karin Gåvsten, coordinator, Stockholm

Private Sessions

"The Possibility of Being Free from Your Past Creates your Future"

This is how I work:
Imagine a gardener at work; he starts by deciding what he wants to create in the garden. Then he weeds and removes big stones, which have been there for years. Then he adds fertile soil and plants the desired plants, trees and bushes he wants growing in his garden. When the basic work is done he can relax waiting for the result, letting nature do the rest.

I will help you get in touch with the primal cause of your problem and release it with my unique mix of NLP, Soulrealignment™, Time Based Techniques and Vortex Healing®. It can be health related or have to do with other areas of your life.

When I was trained in Time Based Techniques I had no idea that I could travel back into my past with the help of my unconscious mind and find specific events, learn from them and be able to use these learnings in my current life, and at the same time let go of all emotional baggage in connection with the event. And that is exactly what happens in a training session. As a result, one experiences that the negative feelings (anger, sorrow, fear, guilt) or the chosen truths are gone forever. A chosen truth can be a "truth" like "I am unworthy", "I cannot make money" or "I am not good enough".

I have witnessed numerous cases where people have released things that have burdened their minds for as long as they can remember.

My first client, an 18-year-old girl had been deeply depressed during the last two years. She had seen various psychologists, but to no avail. Her process had gone so far that she was suicidal. After only a two-hour session (where I was using TLT on her) she felt like she was reborn. I talked to her the next day and she said that the world looked completely different and that for the first time in a long time she could feel happy and expectant about the future.

You can find more information about Time Based Techniques on www.nlpworld.co.uk

Could This Be Something for You?

Read more about the session I offer at www.metamedicine.se

A session is held over the skype (using internet), which means distance isn't a problem.

References

American Journal of Epidemiology 2003;157:415-423, Mars, 2006
Bohr, Niels, Danish Physician, Bohr was the first to use the quantum theory to explain the atom. The model is known as the Bohr atom and for this work Niels Bohr was awarded the Nobel price in physics in 1922.
Cambell Don, The Mozart Effect, Egmont Richter, 2004
Chopra, Deepak, Quantum Healing
Czechmihaley, Mihaley, Flow
Emoto, Masaru, The True Power of Water, Damm, 2004
Fisslinger, Johannes R., Ph.D., President of the META-Health Association, Los Angeles www.metamedicine.info
Hamer, Dr. Ryke Geerd, Summary of the New Medicine, www.thenewmedicine.com
Hay, Louise, Your can heal your life, Hay House
Heidegger, Martin, German philosopher, born 1889–1976, www.heidegger.org
Hicks, Esther and Jerry, Ask and you will receive
Hirneise, Lothar, National Foundation for Alternative Medicine, Washington D.C., author of Chemotherapy Heals Cancer and the World is Flat, published by Sensei / Germany, 2005.
Lillberg, Kirsi, Psychological stress, personality and risk of breast cancer, Follow-up studies in the Finnish Twin Cohort, Helsinki, 2003
Lindquist, Ulla-Karin, Ro utan åror, Nordstedt, 2004
Lipton, Dr. Bruce H., Author of Biology of Belief: Unleashing the Power of Consciousness, Matter and Miracles, earlier Medical professor at University of Neumayr
A and Weiss, W: Liver tumours-new aspects. Hepatogastroenterology 28:1,1981
What the bleep do we know, www.whatthebleep.com/rabbithole/, a popular science film on DVD. It is about quantum physics and how our brain works.

Organ	Brain layer	Conflict	Conflict Phase	Regeneration Phase
Adrenal cortex	CC	Moving in the wrong direction I.G. Not being true to our life purpose	C–, which reduces the cortisol production, stressed fatigue, high blood pressure, Waterhouse Friderichsen Syndrome or Addison's disease	C+, adrenal cysts which produces excess cortisol, Crushing syndrome= increased cortisol level with high energy level, Hirstism= increased body hair even for women
Adrenal medulla	BS	Unstandable stress EG. Life is an unbearable "survival rat-race"	C+, adrenal tumor, hyper tension, increases level of norepinephrine, dopamine and epinephirine	C-, Adrenal stroke
Appendix	BS	Ugly-anger	C+, Tumor in the appendix	C-, appendix inflammation, danger for perforation (bursting)
Bladder – submucosa	BS	Ugly conflict EG. If something felt very ugly	C+, either a secretory or receptory tumor	C- fungus or mycobacteria is helping to break down the tumor
Bladder mucosa	CC	Territory marking EG. Needing to define ones boundary	C- of the bladder mucosa, it can bleed and cause bladder spasms	C+, intense swelling, strong urgency, pain when urinating, reddish urine

Organ	Brain layer	Conflict	Conflict Phase	Regeneration Phase
Blood vessels – arteries & veins	CM	Self-devaluation – disability	C- of the blood vessel walls, normally not noticeable	C+, reparation of the blood vessel walls, swelling, artherioklerosis =stiffening of arteries, atherosclerosis = thinker arteries walls, thrombophlebitis =vein inflammation varices=distended veins
Bones	CM	Self devaluation Conflict content according to the different body parts	C-, osteoporosis, osteolysis = degeneration of bone tissue	C+ reparation, bone cancer, intense anemia at the start, leukemia, joint rheumatism
Breast – ductal	CC	Fear of separation	C- in the milk ducts which causes numbness, slight pain	C+ reparation of the milk ducts, tumor, swelling behind the nipple and the breast itself, inflammation
Breast – mammary glands	Cb	Worry argument or nest conflict	C+ of the mammary glands cells, lobular breast cancer	C- of the tumor, tuberculosis mycobacterium are present to assist the C- process, edema, swelling, pain, if the breast open itself to eliminate the tumor it is stinking

Organ	Brain layer	Conflict	Conflict Phase	Regeneration Phase
Bronchial asthma	CC	Territory fear (motoric cortex) If someone is threatening our territory or wants to leave it without our permission	C- in the bronchial musculature. If more cortex issues are active, then symptoms like wheezing and spasms are present	C+ reparation which causes asthma in the healing crises
Bronchial mucosa	CC	Territory fear (sensoric cortex) Feeling hurt	C- mostly not noticed	C+ coughing,, mucosa, swelling, asthma attack, bronchitis or tumor
Cardiac muscle – myocardium	CM	Being overwhelmed	C- of the cardiac muscle, heart trembling	C+ muscular hypertrophy= enlargement of the heart muscle, heart trembling, high blood pressure, myocardial infarct
Cartilage	CM	Minor self devaluation	C- reduction of cartilage	C+ strengthening of the cartilage, swelling, tumor
Connective tissue	CM	Minor self devaluation	C- of the connective tissue cells	C+ reparation, scars, inflammation
Coronary arteries & veins	CC	Male reaction: Fear of losing the territory Female reaction: Sexual frustration	C- of the wall which increases the blood volume flow and increased power to fight, heart pain, angina pectoris	C+ repairing the walls, swelling, obstruction, heart attack, blood clots

Organ	Brain layer	Conflict	Conflict Phase	Regeneration Phase
Ear – Hearing	CC	Not wanting to hear something	C- loss of the healing ability at the frequency the sound had that we didn't want to hear, it appears like tinnitus	C+, function recovers, hearing loss is possible for some time, edema
Ear – Middle ear	BS	Cannot catch or get rid of a piece of information	C+ flat growing cells, tumor in order to assimilate or eliminate the information better	C- Inflammation of the middle ear, perforation of the tympani is possible
Eye – cornea	CC	Strong visual separation	C- ulcer of the cornea	C+, keratitis= Inflammation of the cornea, edema, pain
Eye – crystalline lens	CC	Visual separation Lost sight of somebody/something	C- necrosis of the lens	C+ reparation, opacity, cataract, enlargement, water inclusion or bending of the lens. Full recovery is possible if the process is chronic the opacity gets stronger every relapse.
Eye – iris	BS	Inability to catch or avoid light particles (Back in the evolution we could eat light particles)	C+, tumor, swelling of the smooth muscle contraction, fixed pupil	C-, iris tuberculosis, coloboma

Organ	Brain layer	Conflict	Conflict Phase	Regeneration Phase
Eye – lachrymal glands	BS	Inability to get rid of something we don't like to see, or the inability to catch something we like to see	C+ of the lachrymal gland, tumor. This helps is to get rid of what we don't like to see or to have a greater chance to get hold of what we like to see	C-, fungus and mycobacteria, encapsulated tumor if the microorganisms aren't present, purulent tears. If the process Is chronic the lachrymal glands can dry up.
Eye – lachrymal glands ducts	CC	To be seen or not like to been seen	C- dilatation of the gland ducts	C+, repairing the gland ducts, swelling, tumor of the gland ducts
Eye – retina	CC	Fear of attack from behind Feeling threatened of something lurking from behind	C-, reduction of vision Near sightedness (introverted person like to hide from the danger), Farsightedness (extroverted persons like to see the danger far away,	C+, edema that can cause a retinal detachment
Eye – vitreous body	CC	Fear of attack Somebody/something is threatening us unexpectedly and frightening us	C-, reduction of vision, vitreous opacity	C+, normalization of the vitreous opacity, glaucoma due to edema, the edema can press thought the entry hole of the optic nerve which can lead to blindness

Organ	Brain layer	Conflict	Conflict Phase	Regeneration Phase
Eye – conjunctiva	CC	Separation – loss Loosing somebody loved or losing sight of him/her	C-, ulcer of the conjunctiva and the eyelid	C+ reparation of the ulcers, conjunctivitis, a redness of the eyelid, pain, itching, burning, loss of eyelashes
Fatty tissue	CM	Minor self devaluation of the part of the body we don't find beautiful	C- of the fatty tissue, mostly not noticed	C+ to repair the tissue, cellulites If this is a chronic process, then the cellulites becomes larger and larger
Gallbladder ducts	CC	Male reaction: Territory anger. Anger about somebody who invades his territory. Female reaction: Feminine identity. Not finding her role within the territory	C- of the bile ducts walls and the gallbladder to improve the bile flowing, pain in the abdomen, bile vomiting and chills	C+ filling the ulcers, higher cholesterol and bile acid, swelling, obstruction of the ducts, hepatitis, hepatic coma, hepatic cirrhosis.
Hair – alopecia	CC	Separation conflict (Same as skin because hair is dead skin cells)	C-, hair loss and decreased sensitivity	C+, but first an intense hair loss, redness in of the skin on the head, then the hair will start to grow again

Organ	Brain layer	Conflict	Conflict Phase	Regeneration Phase
Intestine - small	HS	Indigestible conflict Can't digest something often related to not enough money issue	C+ of cells that produced digestion enzymes for better digestion, tumor	C-, degrading with the help of tuberculosis bacteria, bleedings eliminated with the stool, inflammation, the chronic symptom is called Morbus Chron
Intestine – smooth muscles	HS	Inability to move something forward. Feeling stuck	C- (because the relay is located in the mid brain) reduced peristalsis	C+, increased peristalsis, colic, diarrhea
Kidney – collecting tubules	HS	Existence – abandonment – isolation conflict. Feeling alone, without support, feeling alone in the "desert"	C+, water retention, edema, over-weight, tumor	C- reduction of the renal cells, peeing a lot of "meat smelling" urine, tuberculosis degradation of the tumor, encapsulation, silent kidney, renal collapse, uremia
Kidney – parenchyma	CM	Water conflict Somebody almost drown, was flooded or when you feel like you are drowning in a situation	C- of the renal parenchyma, increases creatine and urea, higher blood pressure, can cause a sclerotic kidney	C+, a cyst forms, becomes part of the kidney and can produce urine, the blood pressure normalize in the end of the regeneration phase

Organ	Brain layer	Conflict	Conflict Phase	Regeneration Phase
Larynx – muscles	CC	Shocking fear	C-, relaxing the larynx in order to improve breathing	C+, regeneration, asthma, difficult to breath, coughing
Larynx – mucosa	CC	Shocking fear or loss of speech conflict	C-, widening the larynx and the voice box in order to improve breathing, slight pain, a slight voice change	C+, swelling of the larynx mucosa, changes in the voice, pressure, tickle in the throat, chronic hoarseness, laryngeal cancer, over sensitive mucosa
Liver parenchyma	HS	Starvation – Existence No money to feed the family, disease diagnose that is threatening the existence	C+, receptory or secretory tumors to help to reabsorb the nutrition and/or digest the nutrition better	C-, degrades though tuberculin micro-bacteria, or it encapsulates or calcifies, tiredness, swelling of the liver, fever, night sweating
Lungs – alveoli	HS	Fear of death	C+ of alveoli cells in order to increase oxygen absorption to be able to fight or flight better for life, tumor	C- with the help of tuberculosis micro-bacteria, without the bacteria the tumor encapsulates
Lymph nodes	CM	Minor self devaluation	C- necrosis in the lymph nodes	C+ reparation, strengthening of the lymph node, swelling, tumor called Hodgkin disease

Organ	Brain layer	Conflict	Conflict Phase	Regeneration Phase
Lymph vessel	CM	Minor self devaluation	C- in the lymph vessel walls in order to increase the lymphatic flow	C+, either swelling, tumor, insufficient lymph drainage or a process without cell proliferation, then the lymph vessels work at full speed in order to break down the congestion
Metabolism – Thalamus	CC	Self-renouncement If only I was dead	C-, restlessness, difficult to fall asleep, changes within the hormonal and blood-chemical parameters	C+, the hormonal and blood-chemical parameters normalize, swelling of thalamus
Mouth	BS	Inability to salivate to get something in or out	C+ resorptive cells of the squamous epithelium grows, in order to improve the ability to salivate and assimilate nutrition or to get it out of the pharynx faster	C- degradation by tuberculosis micro-bacteria or an oral candida

Organ	Brain layer	Conflict	Conflict Phase	Regeneration Phase
Mouth – palate	BS	Inability to get something in or out. Inability to spit something out or inability to swallow it	C+, palate tumor of the old residual intestinal mucosa. This assist to get the "chunk" in or out faster	C- with the help of fungus or micro-bacteria, can stink
Mouth – oral cavity mucosa "blisters"	CC			
Muscles	CM	Minor self devaluation	C-, weaker muscles (muscular atrophy)	C+ rebuilding the muscle (hyper trophia), pain, myosarcoma
Nose – nasal mucosa	CC	Something "stinks" or get strongly on my nerves	C- ulcers in the nasal mucosa, the mucosa gets crusted	C+, swelling, inflammation, running nose, nosebleed
Nose – sinuses mucosa	CC	Something *really* stinks	C- ulcers in the sinuses	C+, intense swelling, with or without viruses, running nose, sinusitis
Oesophagaus - Gullet	BS	Inability to swallow something	C+ in the lower third of oesophagus, tumor	C- tuberculosis is present to degrade the tumor, stinking, varices

Organ	Brain layer	Conflict	Conflict Phase	Regeneration Phase
Ovaries	CM	Profound loss	C-, necrosis of the ovary, reduction of estrogen production, irregular period, amenorrhea	C+, ovarian cyst with the purpose to repair the necrosis. First they are filled with water and later it produces more estrogen which makes the woman look younger. The cyst has a life of 9 months.
Pancreas	BS	Anger – fight – disputes about people, money, objects	C+ of cells producing more pancreatic juice that is more able to digest, tumor, loss of appetite, pain, loss of weight and nausea	C- either the tumor get encapsulated and continue to produce extra pancreatic juice or is degrades with the help of tuberculosis, pancreatic caverns
Pancreas – alpha islet cells	CC	To find someone or something scary disgusting	C-, functional loss of the alpha cells, glucagon insufficiency, blood sugar drops. Normally with sugar cravings	C+, the blood sugar level increases, during the healing crises there is a fast drop of the blood sugar, then it normalizes

Organ	Brain layer	Conflict	Conflict Phase	Regeneration Phase
Pancreas – beta islet cells	CC	Resist or fight against somebody or something	C-, functional loss of the beta cells which lower the insulin production, high blood sugar	C+, the blood sugar level lower itself, during the healing crises there is a high peak of the blood sugar level, then it normalizes
Pancreas mucosa	CC	Male reaction: Territory –anger Female reaction: not finding the feminine identity with in the territory	C-, ulcers in the pancreatic ducts which increases the flow of pancreatic juice	C+, swelling, possible obstruction of the ducts, the amylase of the blood serum is increased, pancreatitis or a pseudo pancreatic tumor
Paralysis	CC	Paralyzing conflict I.G. cannot flee or fight, our way to play dead to survive the threat	C- motor paralysis of the muscles (MS), less or more signals from the motoric center to the skeletal muscles	C+, first there can be more paralysis symptoms, convulsions can arise and the healing crises are epileptic seizures, then the signals normalize
Parathyroid glands	BS	Not being fast enough to get what you desire	C+, with an increase of parathyroidal hormones, which regulates the calcium level in order to increase the muscle contraction	C-, degradation of the tumor by mycobacteria, hormone level normalizes, encapsulation of the tumor is possible, then it continues to produce an increased hormone level

Organ	Brain layer	Conflict	Conflict Phase	Regeneration Phase
Penis	BS	Not being able to penetrate a narrow or dry vagina	C+, increased production of smegma cells	C- with the help of tuberculosis, weeping prepuce
Pericardium	Cb	Attack against the heart – A real one or a perceived one. I.G. A scheduled operation	C+, flat growing cells of the pericardium in order to prevent a danger from the attack	C-, degradation with the help of tuberculosis. After the healing is finished there can be inclusions of calcium.
Peritoneum	Cb	Attack against the abdomen – A real one or a perceived one. IG. A scheduled operation	C+, flat growing cells of the peritoneum in order to prevent a danger from the attack	C-, degradation with the help of tuberculosis. After the healing is finished there can be inclusions of calcium.
Pleura	Cb	Attack against the chest	C+, growing of the pleura in order to prevent a danger from the attack	C-, degradation with the help of tuberculosis. After the healing is finished there can be inclusions of calcium.
Prostate	BS	Not feeling man in his own territory	C+ enlargement of the prostate, higher PSA, pressure on the urethra, a need to urinate often, tumor	C-, PSA normalizes, tumor degrades with help of tuberculosis or it becomes encapsulated, inflammation

Organ	Brain layer	Conflict	Conflict Phase	Regeneration Phase
Rectum – sigma	BS	Ugly – elimination "Can't get the shit out" often is shame, betrayal or bitterness involved	C+, tumor either resorptive or secretory in order to improve digestion	C- degradation of the tumor by tuberculosis, might sweat, bleeding, hemorrhoids
Rectum mucosa	CC	Female reaction: Feminine identity conflict, not knowing where she belongs to, inability to define a position. Male reaction: Territory anger	C- Painful ulceration of the rectum mucosa, hemorrhoids pain	C+, swelling of the mucosa, bleeding, diagnosed as hemorrhoids bleeding or rectum cancer
Renal pelvis mucosa	CC	Can't mark the territory, someone is stepping inside my boundaries	C-, ulcer of the renal pelvis in order to improve the urine flow, minor pains, formation of kidney stones	C+ reparation of the renal pelvis, inflammation, renal colic when the kidney stones get pressed out
Skin – dermis	Cb	Defilement – deformed – identity i.e. feeling someone throwing shit at you, feeling deformed or scared	C+ of the dermis cells to strengthen the dermis, from back heads to skin cancer with or without a mole	C-, reduction of the dermis and the sebum cells, inflammation, acne, tuberculosis of the skin

Organ	Brain layer	Conflict	Conflict Phase	Regeneration Phase
Skin – epidermis	CC	Loss of contact – separation	C- of the outer skin layer. The skin gets pale, poorly supplied with blood, numb and mostly cold	C+ the skin repair itself, becomes red, itchy, swells, eczema
Smell	CC	Can't stand the smell	C-, functional reduction, the smell becomes more and more reduced	C+, at the start the smell can get strongly reduced, then the smelling sense returns
Spermatocyst	CC	Territory – loss – competition Same conflict as the coronary arteries	C- ulcer in the spermatocyst mucosa, which leads to an enlargement or the spermatocyst, in order to be able to store more sperm + an ulcer of the coronary arteries	C+, swelling and inflammation

Organ	Brain layer	Conflict	Conflict Phase	Regeneration Phase
Spleen	CM	Blood loss – conflict	C-, reduction of trombocytes in the spleen. The trombocytes disappear from the peripheral blood-stream in order to avoid blood clots in the blood vessels	C+ reparation of the ulcers in the spleen, enlargement, tumor, the trombocytes rise again
Stomach – duodenum	BS	Inability to digest a situation with anger involved	C+, tumor growing with the intention to increase the resorption of the nutrition	C- tumor degradation with the help of fungus and mycobacteria
Stomach – oesophagus mucosa	CC	Can' swallow something or accept is, like to "spit" is out again	C- Ulcer of the upper 2/3 of the oesophagus	C+, reparation, swelling, difficult to swallow (dysphasia)
Stomach – large curvature	BS	Inability to digest something	C+ of the enzyme cells in order to increase the stomach acid to assist the digestion, tumor	C-, the tumor is reduces with the help of fungus and mycobacteria, inflammation, the stomach acid normalizes, gastritis
Stomach mucosa	CC	Territory anger – disputes	C-, substance loss of the mucosa, pain, spasms, stomach colic and stomach ulcer	C+, bleeding ulcers, vomiting, black stool

Organ	Brain layer	Conflict	Conflict Phase	Regeneration Phase
Teeth bones	CM	Can't bite off in a situation, haven't got the heart to do it, self-devaluation of not being able to bite off	C-, holes inside the teeth bone, the tooth can break, the teeth neck shows longer, the tooth can move and even fall out	C+, reparation, recalcification, swelling, pain, root abscesses
Teeth enamel	CC	Not allowed to bite, defensive	C- caries in the enamel	C+ a slow reparation phase, sensitive to cold/warm and sweet/sour
Tendons	CM	Minor self devaluation	C, necrosis of the tendons, tendon rupture (i.e. Achilles tendon)	C+, refilling the necrosis, swelling, pain
Testicles	CM	Profound loss	C-, necrosis of the interstitial testicles tissue, lower level of testosterone	C+, swelling of the testicle due to the reparation of the tissue, hormone producing cyst
Thyroid – excretory ducts	CC	Feeling powerless	C-, ulcer of the ducts assisting increases flow of thyroxin hormone	C Thyroxin cyst, euthyroid Struma or benign goiter

Organ	Brain layer	Conflict	Conflict Phase	Regeneration Phase
Thyroid glands	BS	Inability to get something or get rid of something	C+, resorptive or secretory tumor, hard sturma, increased metabolism, weight loss and increased appetite, nervousness, hair loss, fatigue, menstrual disorder	C-, the tumor is degrades with the help of mycobacteria, then the hormone level goes back to normal. If it encapsulates ,then the high hormone level persists
Urethral mucosa	CC	Not being able to limit the territory from the inside or mark the limits of the territory	C-, ulcer of the urethral, pain, strong urgency of urination and a painful urination	C+, reparation of the mucosa, swelling, intense urgency and danger of occlusion of the urethra
Uterine tube	BS	An ugly conflict with a man or a masculine woman (half genital)	C+ of the cells that are producing secretion in order to flush the teratoma cells better to the uterus, tumor, obstruction of the uterine tube	C-, degradation with the help of mycobacteria

Organ	Brain layer	Conflict	Conflict Phase	Regeneration Phase
Uterus	BS	Not in contact with the femininity, ugly genital conflict with a man	C+ either a reseptory tumor, which thicken the uterus mucosa so an fertilized egg can better "stick to it" or an secretory tumor with increases the depuration of the uterus	C- the extra cells are eliminated through a heavy period bleeding. If the woman is postmenopausal then the process with take longer time with less bleeding
Uterus – mouth and neck	CC	Sexual frustration conflict, for a masculine woman it will be a loss of territory conflict. (The coronary vein will also be involved)	C-, ulcer of the mouth or neck of uterus, which improves the disposition for a conception. The menstrual period becomes absent	C+, reparation with the help of virus, bleedings, the menstrual cycle will return, can be diagnosed as a tumor
Uterus muscles	BS, but located in the mid brain	Self devaluation of not getting pregnant	C-, necrosis of the uterus muscles	C+ reparation of the muscles, uterine myoma

Organ	Brain layer	Conflict	Conflict Phase	Regeneration Phase
Uterus neck muscle	CC	Self devaluation about not being gable to hold the pregnancy or the penis	C- necrosis of the uterus neck muscle	C+, refilling of the muscle with the help of virus. In the healing crises the sphincter opens (like in the labor) or contracts
Vagina – Bartholini glands	BS	A dry vagina conflict, can't produce enough vaginal mucus for the intercourse	C+ of the cells producing more mucus, tumor	C- the extra cells degrades with the help of tuberculosis, strong smelling vaginal discharge
Vagina mucosa	CC	Not being able or not being allowed to copulate	C- ulcer in the vagina, less sensitivity, spasm, can lead to a vicious circle with difficulties to have an orgasm and lessened libido	C+, repatriation, bleedings the ulcers with a serious flour vaginalis

Printed in Great Britain
by Amazon.co.uk, Ltd.,
Marston Gate.